Couple Corners

52 Faithful Choices for a More Joy-Filled Marriage

By
Paula Whidden

Copyright ©2013 by Paula Whidden

All rights reserved. This book or any portion thereof may not be reproduced or used in any manner whatsoever without the express written permission of the publisher except for the use of brief quotations in a book review.

Printed in the United States of America

Cover design by Jon Bryan
Jonkbryan.Tumblr.com
Photo from istockphoto

First Printing, 2014
Faithful Choices Press
ISBN 9780615941783

Scripture references are from the following sources:

THE HOLY BIBLE, NEW INTERNATIONAL VERSION®, NIV® Copyright © 1973, 1978, 1984, 2011 by Biblica, Inc.® Used by permission. All rights reserved worldwide.

The *Holy Bible*, New Living Translation, copyright ©1996, 2004, 2007 by Tyndale House Foundation. Used by permission of Tyndale House Publishers, Inc., Carol Stream, Illinois 60188. All rights reserved.

Scripture taken from *The Message*. Copyright © 1993, 1994, 1995, 1996, 2000, 2001, 2002. Used by permission of NavPress Publishing Group.

Scriptures and additional materials quoted are from the Good News Bible © 1994 published by the Bible Societies/HarperCollins Publishers Ltd UK, Good News Bible© American Bible Society 1966, 1971, 1976, 1992. Used with permission.

RECOMMENDATIONS FOR *COUPLE CORNERS*

"***Couple Corners*** is an inspiring, insightful and practical guide for not only enhancing your own relationship, but even impacting others. I highly recommend this for all couples whether engaged, newly married, or married for years."

~ **Rusty George,** Lead Pastor of **Real Life Church**, Valencia, CA

"***Couple Corners*** is filled with encouragement and a ton of practical tools to help strengthen your marriage. Paula provides us with a clearer understanding of how Biblical truths can help us navigate the often rough waters of marriage. Whether your marriage is struggling or you are just in need a of a relationship tune up, you will find this book to be inspiring and insightful"

~ **Brandon Beard,** Executive Pastor **Compass Church**, Colleyville TX.

"We live in a culture that continually tears at the very fabric of families and marriages. As a pastor, I'm always looking for great resources to help people. Paula Whidden, in **Couple Corners: 52 Faithful Choices for a More Joy-filled Marriage**, has provided a practical and inspiring book filled with biblical wisdom. I highly recommend it."

~ **Kurt W. Bubna,** Pastor & Author, *Epic Grace* **(Tyndale)**

"All too often couples just are overwhelmed and unable to get started on healing conversations. In this book Paula has provided very simple and quick ways to get to the heart of practices of healthy decisions. By making it easily accessible and fun this book can be a prompt to turn over a few rocks and use them to fashion a lasting foundation."

~ **Jim Beebe,** Marriage and Family Therapist

"I cannot only heartily recommend this devotional, my husband and I will be giving our own 31 year marriage the gift of time next year to further deepen and enrich our relationship. This devotional will do much to open the line of communication to grow, repair and strengthen your marriage. Whether you are a Christian or not, there is much wisdom to be gleaned from Paula's book."

~**DaAnne Smith,** Executive Director, **Single Mothers Outreach**

This book is dedicated to my handsome husband
who always impresses me with his confidence, encouragement,
and passionate faith.
Tim, without you none of this is possible.
You lighten each day just because you're in it.

Contents

Recommendations For Couple Corners 3
Contents 5
Meet the Writer 8
Before you begin 10

First Gear 14
   1. *Seek Sticky Truths* 16
   2. *Think Like a Team* 22
   3. *Be Present* 26
   4. *Believe in Change* 32
   5. *Hang Out With Inspiring Couples* 38
   6. *Have Fun Together* 44
   7. *Walk in Kindness* 50
   8. *Hold Hands* 54
   9. *Bank on Marriage* 60
  10. *Tame the Tongue* 64
  11. *The Dating Dilemma* 68
  12. *Don't Quit Yet* 74

Second Gear 80
  13. *Mind Your Manners* 82

14. Laugh at Yourself	88
15. Serving is Loving	92
16. Follow "The" Role Model	96
17. Set Aside Time for Togetherness	102
18. Beware of Joy Zappers	108
19. Support One Another, Especially When It's Tough	114
20. Give a Shout Out	118
21. Be a Gift Giver	122
22. Sit on the chair	128
23. Take Sage Advice	132
24. Married Not Buried	136

Third Gear 142

25. Pack Some Gear, Expect a Long Ride	144
26. Face Your Fears	148
27. Use Words	154
28. Try, Try Again… In the Bedroom	160
29. Let Go of Self	164
30. Record and Remember the Good	168
31. Communicate Generously	172
32. Keep Envy Out of Your Heart	178
33. Practice Patience	184
34. Harness the Beast of Anger	190
35. Devote Yourself to the Essentials	196
36. Spend Well	200

Fourth Gear 204

37. Dream Big	206

Contents

Recommendations For Couple Corners 3
Contents 5
Meet the Writer 8
Before you begin 10

First Gear 14

1. Seek Sticky Truths 16
2. Think Like a Team 22
3. Be Present 26
4. Believe in Change 32
5. Hang Out With Inspiring Couples 38
6. Have Fun Together 44
7. Walk in Kindness 50
8. Hold Hands 54
9. Bank on Marriage 60
10. Tame the Tongue 64
11. The Dating Dilemma 68
12. Don't Quit Yet 74

Second Gear 80

13. Mind Your Manners 82

14. Laugh at Yourself 88
15. Serving is Loving 92
16. Follow "The" Role Model 96
17. Set Aside Time for Togetherness 102
18. Beware of Joy Zappers 108
19. Support One Another, Especially When It's Tough 114
20. Give a Shout Out 118
21. Be a Gift Giver 122
22. Sit on the chair 128
23. Take Sage Advice 132
24. Married Not Buried 136

Third Gear 142

25. Pack Some Gear, Expect a Long Ride 144
26. Face Your Fears 148
27. Use Words 154
28. Try, Try Again… In the Bedroom 160
29. Let Go of Self 164
30. Record and Remember the Good 168
31. Communicate Generously 172
32. Keep Envy Out of Your Heart 178
33. Practice Patience 184
34. Harness the Beast of Anger 190
35. Devote Yourself to the Essentials 196
36. Spend Well 200

Fourth Gear 204

37. Dream Big 206

38. Be the Needle for Your Rose Bush.. 210
39. Face the Storms Together... 214
40. Refuse to Make Pride Your Buddy... 220
41. Listen Up.. 226
42. Don't Dance for the Devil.. 232
43. Count the Pluses.. 236
44. Remove Rude from the 'Tude.. 240
45. Forgive often... 244
46. Back Off the Boasting Words... 250
47. Hang Onto the Rope of Hope.. 254
48. Breeze It, Buzz It, Easy Does It... 258

Fifth Gear...264

49. Learn the Secret.. 266
50. Be The Good Wife... 272
51. Be the Good Husband.. 278
52. Make God the Center of Your Marriage..................................... 284

Reverse...290

Meet the Writer

This book began 35 years ago. My parents struggled to keep their flailing marriage together and decided it wouldn't work. They began the process for divorce. Sitting at center field, I saw it all.

I hadn't lived with both parents for quite a while. Dad kept an apartment and a girlfriend on the side. Mom worked hard to take care of me and my brother. This may be common for many people now, but as I grew up, I knew no one with separated parents.

One weekend, as my brother and I helped my dad relocate items to his new apartment, we became victims of a car accident. My brother and I survived, our Dad didn't. It was one thing to imagine growing up in a divorced home and another to be the child of a widow in a world full of couples.

My strong Mom brought me up to trust Christ in every arena of life. She committed herself to providing us with godly role models. That's when this book began.

At the time, everywhere I looked (books, movies, television shows) displayed strong couple after strong couple. I desperately wanted to know, dream, and live this reality. Thus began an obsession observing the people and marriages in my life.

Searching for reasons people stick in their marriages and why they separated became a passion I have carried to this day. I've discovered that people make choices in marriage as if they were turning corners on the road of life..

If life were a road trip, the corners we take either lead us closer to or further from our desired destination. The more corners I saw people turn, the more I noticed how their choices brought them closer to each other or further apart as a couple.

In 1996, I received my Master's of Divinity at Fuller Theological seminary because of how much I noticed the strength people got when they placed their faith in Christ. Before and after that time, I have actively ministered to individuals and families for more than 20 years in various roles including premarital counseling and marriage mentoring.

I created a blog called *Faithful Choices* a couple of years ago, because I believe our faith affects our choices and our choices affect our faith.

It is my prayer that these choices help you to grow closer to Christ and closer as a couple.

Sincerely,

Paula Whidden

Before you begin

Recall that moment on a road trip with your spouse, when you reach a corner and one of you calls out, "Turn left." The other shakes his head and says, "No, it's right."

If you were in separate vehicles, you would part ways and check out your own destination. This is a couple corner.

As you read this book, you will discover 52 uniquely different corners we encounter as couples. These choices are not little stories, though some include stories. They are observations based on my obsession with healthy relationships.

While you could certainly read through it in a few days, if you slow down to read and absorb one choice a week, you will receive the best benefit from this book.

I encourage you to take the time to fully appreciate and encounter one corner a week. As you do, you'll discover the joy God intended you to have within marriage. The best way to get access to this joy comes when both of you read and choose together, but one person making an effort to grow and change does matter.

There is no time constraint. Pull up to the corner. Think about it. Let its full impact seep into your soul. You can go in order, or pick and choose. Bookmark the ones you know will require more time, there's nothing wrong with returning later to continue the growth.

If you prefer to take the corners in their original order, I've split them up into groups based on speed, difficulty, and the difference they will make in your marriage. We begin with the most comfortable corners, which is why I call this section first gear. By the time you reach the end, if you're a brave enough driver, you'll be speeding down the highway of marriage in fifth gear. This one moves you forward the fastest, but also contains the biggest risks.

When you are ready, turn over the engine, pop the clutch, and shift gears.

Following each corner, you'll see a list of similar corners. If you desire to continue learning further within the topic go ahead.

families for more than 20 years in various roles including premarital counseling and marriage mentoring.

I created a blog called *Faithful Choices* a couple of years ago, because I believe our faith affects our choices and our choices affect our faith.

It is my prayer that these choices help you to grow closer to Christ and closer as a couple.

Sincerely,

Paula Whidden

Before you begin

Recall that moment on a road trip with your spouse, when you reach a corner and one of you calls out, "Turn left." The other shakes his head and says, "No, it's right."

If you were in separate vehicles, you would part ways and check out your own destination. This is a couple corner.

As you read this book, you will discover 52 uniquely different corners we encounter as couples. These choices are not little stories, though some include stories. They are observations based on my obsession with healthy relationships.

While you could certainly read through it in a few days, if you slow down to read and absorb one choice a week, you will receive the best benefit from this book.

I encourage you to take the time to fully appreciate and encounter one corner a week. As you do, you'll discover the joy God intended you to have within marriage. The best way to get access to this joy comes when both of you read and choose together, but one person making an effort to grow and change does matter.

There is no time constraint. Pull up to the corner. Think about it. Let its full impact seep into your soul. You can go in order, or pick and choose. Bookmark the ones you know will require more time, there's nothing wrong with returning later to continue the growth.

If you prefer to take the corners in their original order, I've split them up into groups based on speed, difficulty, and the difference they will make in your marriage. We begin with the most comfortable corners, which is why I call this section first gear. By the time you reach the end, if you're a brave enough driver, you'll be speeding down the highway of marriage in fifth gear. This one moves you forward the fastest, but also contains the biggest risks.

When you are ready, turn over the engine, pop the clutch, and shift gears.

Following each corner, you'll see a list of similar corners. If you desire to continue learning further within the topic go ahead.

After a bit, we will progress through second, third and fourth gears. Only a few couples will get to fifth gear. Adventurous risk takers who believe in the impossible possibility of lifelong joyfilled marriages can and will speed past those too fearful to try. It isn't for the shy or tame of heart, it's a high speed, don't let the cops catch you kind of ride.

Couple Corners is an ongoing work in progress. You are invited to make suggestions and submit further corners you've encountered. I'd love to hear your road trip tales.

Please send your suggestions or comments to paula@faithfulchoices.com.

As you begin this marital adventure, may I pray for you?

Lord God,

Thank you for this person who has opened this book and wants to grow in their marriage. Let their marriage grow stronger and closer to You. Enable them to find the joy You have for them today and every week as they encounter these corners. No matter where they've come from or what they've seen within their lives, help them to know You are stronger than their past. You have a plan for their future.

In Jesus' beautiful name we pray,

Amen

"Men occasionally stumble over the truth,
but most of them pick themselves up and hurry off
as if nothing ever happened."
~Winston Churchill

FIRST GEAR

If you want to begin any trip, you first get the car rolling. These first twelve corners lay a foundation for the rest. They ignite our marital engine and the propel us forward.

"Men occasionally stumble over the truth,
but most of them pick themselves up and hurry off
as if nothing ever happened."
~Winston Churchill

First Gear

If you want to begin any trip, you first get the car rolling. These first twelve corners lay a foundation for the rest. They ignite our marital engine and the propel us forward.

1. SEEK STICKY TRUTHS

I met a couple who had been married 70 years. Can you imagine that, 70 years?

One Sunday, they watched me and my boyfriend in church. After the service, they approached us. Lewis, the husband, said, "We saw you holding hands. We love it too." They held up their clinging hands to prove his point.

Not what I pictured when I thought of long-term marriage. I guess I assumed people become used to each other's company. I assumed they stop making an effort to connect.

Some couples stop trying, but not Lewis and Mary Beth.

How did they do it?

One day, I approached the wife in this couple, Mary Beth, and asked her for advice on how to stick together for the long haul. She told me, she never said any words to damage their friendship. Their friendship?

I didn't know couples could or should be friends. My parents definitely weren't friends.

My parents struggled in marriage. When I was 10 years old they had decided to end their marriage. One week prior to beginning divorce proceedings, my dad died in a car accident. Mom remained single. As a result, I developed a passionate desire to understand how couples stick.

I sought advice from friends with marriages I respect. I asked what marriage felt like and what they experienced. They taught me their sticky truths.

The sticky marital truths:
- Friendship lasts longer than romance.
- Romance adds icing to the friendship cake.
- There are times when neither romance nor friendship keeps a couple strong.

When couples lean on God's love, He anchors them in life's troubled waters.

As Tim (the boyfriend) and I grew more serious, I shared with him my dream. A relationship where I could say, "I love him, I like him and I'm in love with him."

It looked something like this:
I love him (the way God wants all humans to love one another).
I like him (as my best friend).

I'm in love with him (the romantic spark lives and burns in our lives).

Mary Beth and Lewis enjoyed this kind of marriage. When she and I spoke, she told me of times when she felt less than romantic. We all get tired, even the cutest guy loses his brilliance in regular day-to-day moments. Frankly, so do the cute girls.

She liked Lewis, her husband. They held hands, talked and shared life. She also told me sometimes she didn't like him. On those days, she held her tongue and practiced loving him as God wants us to love all people.

She never regretted having said the wrong thing. And, it worked for them for 70+ years. Not all of us can say the same thing about our marriages, but that doesn't mean we can't start seeking to be better friends from this point forward.

Tim and I eventually married. We aspire to go the long haul just like Mary Beth and Lewis. We continue to seek couples who've done this marriage thing longer than us. They provide us with guidance and support.

Growth Questions:

- Do you know any couples who have been married a long time? What questions could you ask them about their marriage?

- If you don't know a couple who inspire you, how can you find them?

- What sticky truths have you observed in longtime couples?

Bible verses on this topic:

"So again I say, each man must love his wife as he loves himself, and the wife must respect her husband." Ephesians 5:33 (NLT)

"Then you will know the truth, and the truth will set you free."
John 8:32 (NIV)

Similar choices:

#5 Hang Out with Inspiring Couples

#50 Be the Good Wife

#51 Be the Good Husband

2

2. Think Like a Team

Growing up, I watched and participated in many different kinds of teams: football, baseball, hockey, soccer, basketball, cycling, etc. Do you watch sports or participate in one?

Don't worry; you don't have to compete to understand this choice.

In every sport, we find givers and takers. The takers are showboats who take the spotlight away from the other players. The givers include those generous, inclusive players everyone wants to emulate.

If you're watching football, you know it only takes one persistent guy to slam a quarterback to the ground. Famous quarterbacks, like Joe Montana, have the back surgery scars to prove it. When Joe's team fought for him, they all won. When he acted uppity and didn't respect their efforts, he got slammed.

2

2. Think Like a Team

Growing up, I watched and participated in many different kinds of teams: football, baseball, hockey, soccer, basketball, cycling, etc. Do you watch sports or participate in one?

Don't worry; you don't have to compete to understand this choice.

In every sport, we find givers and takers. The takers are showboats who take the spotlight away from the other players. The givers include those generous, inclusive players everyone wants to emulate.

If you're watching football, you know it only takes one persistent guy to slam a quarterback to the ground. Famous quarterbacks, like Joe Montana, have the back surgery scars to prove it. When Joe's team fought for him, they all won. When he acted uppity and didn't respect their efforts, he got slammed.

In a choir—a different type of team and one of my favorites—all voices must join together in tone and intensity of volume, no one sound should ring louder than another. In the perfect blend of voices, the choir finds its success.

Whatever type of team you understand best, the math works the same. A team requires team work to succeed. Because of this coaches often shout, "There's no 'I' in team!"

I remember the first time I realized the teamwork required in marriage.

Tim and I had become engaged. We flew out to visit his family in Michigan. His parents had already been married 30+ years.

While driving to visit some other family members, Tim's mom and dad had a dispute in the front seat of the car, while we observed their conversation from behind.

They each held a vastly different view on the topic they discussed. They exchanged their ideas, then, my now mother-in-law said something like, "Look, we're a team, and we're going to work together on this; that's what we do."

It felt as if a light bulb plugged itself into my head and lit up the backseat.

They'd been married so long, because when they disagreed, they still wanted to work together. I made a mental note.

Growth Questions:

- Have you ever considered your marriage like a team? What sort of team do you understand best?

- What types of sacrifices have you or your spouse made to help your team work?

- How could you challenge yourself to be more sacrificial?

Bible verses on this topic

"Submit to one another out of reverence for Christ." Ephesians 5:21 (NIV)

"Two people are better off than one, for they can help each other succeed." Ecclesiastes 4:9 (NLT)

Similar choices

#5 Hang Out with Inspiring Couples

#17 Set Aside Time for Togetherness

#29 Let Go of Self

3

3. Be Present

At work, when we network to build connections with our co-workers, our focused presence improves the work experience. When we play with our children or express interest in their school and what they do, our presence encourages them.

Being present improves friendships, business contacts, conversational success, enjoyment of hobbies, sports, and more.

A distracted mind or absent heart creates a rift which, unless addressed, becomes a chasm separating you from each other. Imagine watching the Grand Canyon form in fast forward. While it is beautiful in its enormity, its too big of an expanse for anyone to build a bridge.

Jonah works from 8am-6pm at a restaurant. He stands on his feet all day. When he meets up with his wife Tara at the end of the day, he's exhausted. So is she.

She teaches second graders, and then picks up their elementary school-aged daughter and teenage son at the end of the school day. When they arrive home, she finishes her own school work while helping her kids finish their homework. At this point, her homework begins. She cleans, cooks, and organizes around the house.

By the time Jonah and she see each other; they each need a break from life. He goes into the bedroom to play a couple of games on his tablet. She sits down in front of the television.

Their precious together time is spent separately.

Tara finds herself getting frustrated with Jonah. Over time, huge differences develop between them due to mental and physical absence. She tells her friends of the problems, but not Jonah.

A chasm forms in their relationship.

When was the last time they shared their thoughts together?

When did he last ask her, "What does marriage mean to you?" Had he ever? Had she ever asked him? The question is worth asking.

To allow this question to have traction, they decide to agree, believing there are no wrong answers.

They sit down at the kitchen table to talk. They take time for each to share 10 things they care about most in their marriage.

If the same problem plagues your marriage, you could do the same.

After sharing, mutually decide to pick the three things that matter most. (Some couples might feel one thing is more than enough.) Then, choose to focus on improving those things throughout this year.

Here are ideas to get started. Every couple's list will be different.

What matters most in our marriage?

- Time to talk one-on-one
- Dates
- Doing chores together (that's right, chores)
- Sex/affection/touching
- Agreement on money
- Respect
- Controlling Anger
- Shared Time
- Fun
- Shared Faith/Beliefs
- Skiing
- Underwater pumkin carving *(Just checking if you were paying attention.)*
- Animal rescue
- Exercise
- Reading
- Entertainment (i.e. movies, videos, etc.)

Did you notice that these examples don't include stuff about the children? As much as we all adore our kids, the marriage is the foundation for the family. It has to come first. Whether they say it or not, our kids are counting on this foundation.

Once we determine each others needs and interests, we can prioritize better. We begin building bridges capable of spanning any previous chasm.

Only if we pay attention to each other's needs and stay present in our minds and hearts will we be ready and available to pick each other up when necessary.

Growth Questions:

- In what ways have you experienced difficulty being fully present with your spouse?

- What can you do to change this pattern?

- Which elements of marriage matter most to you? To your spouse?

- Which one or ones will you and your spouse decide to work on now?

Bible verses on this topic:

"Two are better than one, because they have a good return for their labor: If either of them falls down, one can help the other up. But pity anyone who falls and has no one to help them up." Ecclesiastes 4:9-10 (NIV)

"So encourage each other and build each other up, just as you are already doing." 1 Thessalonians 5:11 (NIV)

Similar choices:

#2 Think Like a Team

#11 The Dating Dilemma

#28 Try, Try Again… in the Bedroom

4

4. Believe in Change

What we believe about ourselves and those we love makes a difference.

Have you ever felt like you were incapable of breaking the cycles of the past? Or maybe you believed your husband or wife was incapable? Like nothing new would ever happen. As a result, you limited your expectation of yourself and them.

We all have failings. With God's help anyone can change, anyone can improve. Do you believe this?

When it comes to our failings, we often assume we cannot improve or alter an action we've done for years. God has a different perspective.

I grew up in a predominately single parent home. By the time my dad died, he hadn't lived within our home for quite a while. In fact, I have no clear recollection of his daily at-home involvement, except a few fights.

When I found Tim, I wondered how I could even relate to marriage. I hadn't seen it work in a first-hand sort of way. To be fair, God had been preparing me without my knowledge. In my obsession to observe content and joyous couples, He had given me more knowledge than I realized.

Still, I have faced many personal road blocks in regard to my view of wifely and husbandly roles. It bothered me to put myself within some simple wifey box and cow-down to the man of my life. No Way! And yet, God has lovingly guided my heart toward changed attitudes about myself and marriage as a whole.

Before I continue, I should give you some information. The simple "wifey" box I envisioned felt like a trap. The truth of learning to become a loving wife makes me feel free.

Many of us feel trapped by our past or our own self-imposed images of life. The same happens when anyone struggles with a life-pattern they long to change. Whether it's alcoholism, abuse, hoarding, pornography, overeating, disbelief in God, or some image of marriage stuck in our brains, what we trust in these circumstances will affect any change we desire.

The Apostle Paul refers to his own failings this way:

"I want to do what is good, but I don't. I don't want to do what is wrong, but I do it anyway." Romans 7:19 (NLT)

Have you ever felt stuck in a never changing cycle you cannot stop?

You know the old expression, "You can't teach an old dog new tricks." (I'm not referring to any of us as the "old dog," you'll see what I mean.) Many of us assume an expression that has been around so long must contain truth.

A couple of years ago, my husband and I spent a week teaching our 13 year old dog to enjoy sleeping in a crate for the first time in her life. It took only a week. This old dog, which had previously slept on our king-sized bed beside us, learned something new the year before she passed away from old age, and she enjoyed it.

We also establish certain habits in our marriages. Then, we assume we cannot change because we've practiced them too long. God longs to make us a new creation. He has a plan to change us in the best possible way.

If we want improvement within our lives, within our marriages, we need to believe He can do what He says He will do.

As we read the Bible, doing our best to follow what it says, we seek to learn from people who've experienced God's miraculous works first hand. One day we will look back and realize how much our lives have changed. We've become a new person with new ideas and the old is gone.

Do you struggle with these same fears? May you find encouragement.

Keep trusting Him and following Him and seeking His will. He will surprise you with His ability no matter where we've been in the past or what we've done.

You may need to bring in outside help like a counselor, marriage therapist or addiction advocate. It's tough to choose to submit to someone else as we seek change, yet this humbled attitude is the sweet spot of faith with God. When we set aside our fears and believe in His possibilities, anything is possible.

If you are the one in need of change, begin praying for God's guidance to give you strength and encouragement as you seek to become who He means you to be. If your spouse has issues yet to face, pray for God to open his or her eyes to see the problem and be willing to face it. Also ask God for patience as you trust His timing on this issue.

Growth Questions:

- Do you or your spouse have a problem or doubt which needs to be addressed? How has this issue kept you from growing as a couple?

- Have you witnessed God's ability to change someone else? What did it look like?

- What are steps you could take today to begin believing in the change He has for you?

Bible verses on this topic:

"No, in all ths things we have complete victory through him who loved us! For I am certain that nothing can separate us from his love: neither death nor life, neither angels nor other heavenly rulers or powers, neither the present nor the future, neither the world above nor the world below—there is nothing in all creation that will ever be able to separate us from the love of God which is ours through Christ Jesus our Lord." Romans 8:37-39 (GNT)

"But if we hope for what we do not yet have, we wait for it patiently. In the same way, the Spirit helps us in our weakness." Romans 8:25-26a (NIV)

Similar choices:

#52 Make God the Center of Your Marriage
#12 Don't Quit Yet
#22 Sit on the Chair

5

5. Hang Out With Inspiring Couples

Inspiration can come from any direction. It's an idea, a picture, a thought, a dream, a person. We need inspiration in our lives.

Without people to inspire us, we'd still all use fire places for heat. We'd dress in brown and never cut our hair. Without inspiration, the great inventions of our time would never have happened.

Consider this:
- Steve Jobs had Edwin H. Land (the guy who created instant photography).
- Laser inventor Gordon Gould was inspired by Thomas Edison.
- Albert Einstein found inspiration in the music of Mozart.

➢ Oprah received encouragement and strength from her 4th grade teacher, Mary Duncan.

With these people in mind, let's consider how much inspiration we need to make our marriages successful.

Who inspires you in your marriage?

We need people who open our eyes to the possibilities God has already created. To do it, we need other couples around us who help our imaginations go farther than our experiences.

Webster's dictionary defines inspiration this way:

Inspiration:

- A divine influence or action on a person believed to qualify him or her to receive and communicate sacred revelation
- the action or power of moving the intellect or emotions
- the act of influencing or suggesting opinions

Years ago, people around us were sticking like glue but it isn't so these days. We have to hunt if we want inspiration.

Committed couples need other committed couples for the same reasons that doctors talk with doctors, artists observe other artists and writers read other people's stories.

Where to start?

If you aren't sure where to find inspiring couples, may I suggest church. With eyes wide open, observe the couples who attend church. How do they treat one another? How do they talk about each other or to each other? If you don't attend a church, it's time to start. When hunting for Christian marriage mentors, it's like Grand Central Station.

Be aware, not every couple will fit the bill. Let's consider that if you attend church and you are seeking someone as an example, you may not consider yourself an example. The same is true for other couples. But when you readily seek, you will find.

Ask God to give you the eyes to see strong couples when they cross your path, He will enable you to develop laser point vision.

Growth Questions:

- Where do you find inspiration to strengthen your marriage?

- Which definition of inspiration caught your attention most?

- Do you know any other couples you admire? What kind of things could you learn from them?

Bible verses on this topic:

"Plans go wrong for lack of advice; many advisers bring success." Proverbs 15:22 (NLT)

"… let the wise listen and add to their learning, and let the discerning get guidance" Proverbs 1:5 (NIV)

Similar choices:

#23 Take Sage Advice

#1 Seek Sticky Truths

#25 Pack Some Gear, Expect a Long Ride

6

6. Have Fun Together

Do you remember the fun you had when you were dating your husband or wife? What memories stand out?

Have you ever laughed together so hard you almost peed your pants?

I think about the time Tim and I went to a museum. We had planned to go to the beach, but when morning came it was pouring down rain. Without hesitation Tim said, "Let's do plan B." I had no idea what plan B was.

We ended up going to a museum, then the restaurant next door. We had a blast! We made fun of the pictures. We watched the people examining the art. And we made a point of kissing in front of the surveillance cameras. I'll bet you have memories like this which always bring a smile to your face when you remember them.

Fun and laughter matter to us on a deeply personal level. We value it so much entire industries have developed for the purpose of milking that need dry.

If we didn't long for fun and laughter, there would be…
- No amusement parks
- No comedians
- No adventure vacation planners
- No baseball, hockey, tennis, cycling, basketball, etc.
- No theater
- No circuses
- No video games
- No zoos
- No movies

Think of how much money we put into any of these things. Fun and laughter still matter.

Each couple determines their own definition of fun. The Star Wars couples create amazing costumes and dress up. Some couples climb mountains, some play Frisbee, some watch "Gomer Pyle" on TV because old is so retro and cool these days. Some couples play board games, some play video games, and some cook or sew or paint. However you define fun, do it together, and you'll connect more.

If we giggle our hardest, chest-pounding giggles together joined in heart and mind, when tough stuff happens, we can talk about the scary, deep, serious stuff too.

There is one important catch to this approach. We cannot strictly share our kind of fun; we must also share in what lights up our husband or wife. It's a sacrifice, but they are worth it.

My grandmother wasn't a hockey fan, until she married my grandfather. Because she adored him, she attended the games. To make it fun for herself, she purposely rooted for the opposing team he supported, and she waited for fights. That's right, my four foot eleven inch, wheelchair bound grandmother discovered she found it fun to watch those big guys move slowly on the ice and yank on each other's clothes, while swinging hockey sticks back and forth.

Grandpa loved the game and Grandma found fun in certain moments. Together, they laughed.

He also participated in a fun hobby of hers, being a resort tourist. They lived in Phoenix, Arizona, home to some gorgeous resorts. She adored the beauty of these spaces, and he tagged along. Actually, he drove. I did mention she was in a wheelchair, right?

He discovered an ability to guide visiting friends to great places for vacation. After all, he had already visited the best places in town. Grandpa discovered he liked being "in-the-know."

Did I mention, they were married over 50 years?

Growth Questions:

- What fun memories pop into your mind as you read this choice?

- What made those memories fun?

- How can you continue to experience fun and create memories in your marriage today? Make a plan to do it.

Bible verses on this topic:

"Come, let's drink deeply of love till morning; let's enjoy ourselves with love!" Proverbs 7:18 (NIV)

"Dear friend, I pray that you may enjoy good health and that all may go well with you, even as your soul is getting along well." 3 John 1:2 (NIV)

"It is good to be able to enjoy the pleasant light of day." Ecclesiastes 11:7 (GNT)

Similar choices:

#14 Laugh at Yourself

#30 Record and Remember the Good

#37 Dream Big

7

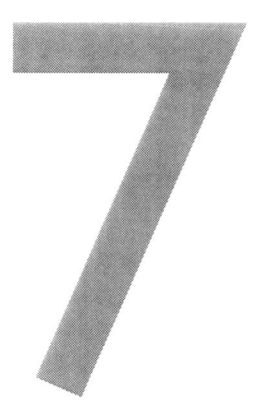

7. Walk in Kindness

Desmond and Corina pass each other every day within their home hardly exchanging any words. They've been married for 15 years and feel as if they've already said it all. At some point, they became so accustomed to one another they stopped being purposely kind to one another.

Desmond always teases Corina about her insecurities like her weight and her lack of cooking skills. Corina gives the courtesy chuckle, but it hurts every time. In response, Corina never stops pointing out how she makes more money than Desmond. He refuses to acknowledge how much pain this stirs in him.

Their lack of kindness toward each other acts like a small rip in a piece of fabric. As they each tug on it, they grow further and further apart.

We show and live kind lives through our tone of voice, our expressions, our attitudes, our opinions, and our actions. If we know what kindness is when we receive it, we can challenge ourselves to be the kindness starters in our own home.

Many people love giving a random act of kindness to a stranger, but what about those people we see and live with every day. They need continual kindness, not random moments.

Growth Questions:

- How do you express kindness toward your spouse? Is there room for improvement?

- Is your spouse kind to you? How does it make you feel?

- You cannot change your spouse but you can change you. What could you do today to begin acting more kindly toward him or her?

Bible verses on this topic:

"Therefore, as God's chosen people, holy and dearly loved, clothe yourselves with compassion, kindness, humility, gentleness and patience."
Colossians 3:12 (NIV)

"If it is possible, as far as it depends on you, live at peace with everyone."
Romans 12:18 (NIV)

Similar choices:

#33 Practice Patience

#45 Forgive Often

#43 Count the Pluses

8

8. Hold Hands

Jeremy leans back in the couch; he slouches shoulder to shoulder with Lynnette. It's their third date.

As they enjoy the movie, the tops of their hands brush past one another. He feels his desires stir while the fear of rejection peers over his shoulder. She wonders if she should clasp his hand first or wait for him to grab hers. Sitting on the edge of the most exhilarating tingling sensation, they bask in this wondrous moment.

Lynnette never imagined something as small and subtle as a hand touch could stir her senses in this magical way, but the anticipation and desire she feels speaks volumes. She wants this simple touch more than she ever imagined she would.

Jeremy and Lynnette softly let their fingers entwine; a smooth, gentle lighting flashes between them, the magnetism of the moment draws them to one another without force or insistence but with respect and mutual desire.

Maybe you can relate, because you felt the same way when you first touched the hand of your spouse. Perhaps you find this odd, because you've never really spent much time holding hands.

Unlike a kiss, hand holding can be done through fatigue, illness, invasive relatives and much more. The caring and compassionate linking of palms brings flirtation and sensuality in an unexpected way.

In 2006, the University of Virginia held experiments on the value of hand holding to calm a stressful moment. They placed electrodes on the ankles of self-proclaimed happily married women and gave them mild shocks while reading their brain activity. *(Yeah, I know. I probably wouldn't have volunteered for this experiment, but we can still learn from these brave women.)*

The women received one shock without anyone nearby, one while holding the hand of a stranger, and one while holding the hand of their spouse. They rated their discomfort during the experimentation while researchers observed their brain waves. Holding the hand of a stranger helped to relieve the stress a bit, but holding the hand of a beloved spouse helped much more.

The researchers saw a definite difference in brain activity between hand holding and going it alone. They even noticed the improved value of hand holding for happy couples over the clasp of a stranger.

In October 2011, *Time* magazine exposed us to a couple who had been married for 72 years. They both ended up in the ICU of a hospital in Des Moines, Iowa as a result of a severe car accident. While there, they held hands.

Gordon, 94, died while in ICU, but his family noticed a heartbeat on the monitor in spite of his lack of breath. The heartbeat came from Norma, 90, whose hand remained clasped to his. She passed away while still holding his hand more than an hour later.

Their family appreciated the beauty of their ending.

If this idea is new to you, here are ways to create a lasting connection by linking fingers.

Remember

to

F.L.I.R.T.

F lexibility matters.

Remaining in the same position can interfere with a flirty hand hold. By re-adjusting the grip on a regular basis, we keep the flirtation going.

L inger.

When a couple watches a movie together, attends church, goes to a restaurant or walks down the street, little lingering touches build the flirtation. Brush past one another gently, laying one hand on top of another. Quick, soft grab-and-go moments allow a little lingering and create a spark which eventually seeks a fire.

I nitiative.

Someone has to reach out first, why not you? If you make no effort, you'll receive no reward. Hand holding is a joy unto itself for both men and women.

R emember the three bears.

Not too soft, not too hard, we're looking for just right. Too soft, also known as Jello fingers, feels like we aren't really interested. Too hard, the business handshake, feels too forceful. Finding the balance helps us to clasp our loved one's hand with the proper amount of pressure.

T ouch with tenderness.

Holding a hand while stroking the palm or calmly caressing the tips of the fingers brings a sweetness and unforced strength to the hand-holding experience.

F.L.I.R.T. with your spouse by holding hands. As we seek joy and contentment in marriage, we can measure its strength by the connection between our palms.

If you've never spent much time holding your spouse's hand, why not give it a try? Try it for a month and see what you discover.

Growth Questions:

- How often do you and your spouse hold hands?

- What do you like or not like about the hand-holding experience?

- Share your feelings with one another. How does your spouse feel about hand holding? Decide to try it for a month to see how it affects your relationship.

Bible verses on this topic:

"Again the one who looked like a man touched me and gave me strength."
Daniel 10:18 (NIV)

"—for whoever touches you touches the apple of his eye"
Zechariah 2:8b (NIV)

Similar choices:

#15 Serving is Loving

#11 The Dating Dilemma

#43 Count the Pluses

9

9. Bank on Marriage

Let's think through a scenario.

You know you have money in the bank. You drive up to the ATM and withdraw some of your money. You use that same ATM debit card at store after store to buy several little things.

Then, one day you stop in at Starbucks after a particularly hard day. You feel as if life itself will end if you don't purchase your favorite Mocha Frappacchino. You hand your faithful plastic card to the lady behind the cash register. She tells you the card has been declined.

Can you guess what happened?

You pulled out money from your account, but failed to deposit more into the bank.

Imagine a marriage relationship is like a bank account.

Whenever we criticize or attack our spouse, we make a withdrawal. Whenever we affirm or encourage our spouse, we make a deposit.

When we make more deposits and fewer withdrawals, we feel more secure in our relationship as does our spouse.

To keep the marriage strong, we must encourage one another more than we discourage one another.

Growth Questions:

- What happens if we withdraw more than we deposit?

- Do you tend to make more deposits or more withdrawals?

- What can you do to make more deposits to your marital bank account?

Bible verses on this topic:

"May the God who gives endurance and encouragement give you the same attitude of mind toward each other that Christ Jesus had," Romans 15:5 (NIV)

"Remember this—a farmer who plants only a few seeds will get a small crop. But the one who plants generously will get a generous crop."
2 Corinthians 9:6 (NLT)

"Therefore encourage one another and build each other up, just as in fact you are doing." 1 Thessalonians 5:11 (NIV)

Similar choices:

#32 Keep Envy Out of Your Heart

#31 Communicate Generously

#29 Let Go of Self

10

10. Tame the Tongue

The mouth, what a monstrously powerful projector of the heart!

In comparison to other parts of our bodies, the tongue occupies a small space. Yet, through the way we use it, we can create either great joy or overwhelming trouble.

I grew up loving a good argument. My brother and I could argue over anything, regardless of whether we actually knew what we were talking about. But in retrospect, I've discovered how it traps us in an attack and defend mode that doesn't produce any real connection.

Just because I can talk louder or more forcibly doesn't mean I've changed someone's mind. It usually means they became wise enough to stop the conversation from their side. The more I argue my point of view, the more they mentally dig into their point of view. Arguments rarely produce change.

As parents we often tell our children to "use their words," but the right words at the right moment mean so much more than just any old word at any old moment.

If you struggle with this issue too, here are some quotes I found on the topic of arguments: (I hope they help you.)

> Never argue with a fool, onlookers may not be able to tell the difference. ~Author unknown, attributed to Mark Twain

> I just wish my mouth had a backspace key. ~Author Unknown

> Not even the fastest horse can catch a word spoken in anger. ~Chinese Proverb

> Speak when you are angry and you will make the best speech you will ever regret. ~Ambrose Bierce

> Silence is one of the hardest arguments to refute. ~Josh Billings

Saying what we want in the moment not only causes problems, it can drive a wedge between couples. This sort of separation remains long after the argument. It sticks in the brain like silly putty on carpeting. No matter how hard you try, a remnant glues itself in place for years to come.

Many grandmas have said over the years, "If we cannot say anything good, we shouldn't say anything at all." Those grandmas were married a long time, perhaps they knew something.

Growth Questions:

- Do you remember any negative words someone said to you from your childhood? Have they remained stuck in your head over the years?

- How can you prevent yourself from saying the wrong thing at the wrong time to the person you love most in this world?

- Has your spouse said something you still feel glued inside your brain? What was it? You can choose to forgive them now for their words of the past.

Bible verses on this topic:

"Too much talk leads to sin. Be sensible and keep your mouth shut." Proverbs 10:19 (NLT)

"May these words of my mouth and this meditation of my heart be pleasing in your sight, LORD, my Rock and my Redeemer." Psalm 19:14 (NIV)

Similar choices:

#31 Communicate Generously

#41 Listen Up

#46 Back off Boasting Words

Couple Corners: 52 Faithful Choices for a More Joy-Filled Marriage

11. The Dating Dilemma

Have you heard the mantra being spouted by many well-meaning marriage counselors?

Be sure to have date nights.

The idea of this causes Emily's stomach to rumble. It just isn't an option. They both work, but the credit cards are maxed. Family lives three states away. She and Jeremiah work hard at keeping their marriage strong, but they simply cannot do date nights.

It's not like they've wasted their money. They've cutback everywhere they can imagine, but it's still tight.

What's a couple to do?

I'm not against couples dating one another. As a matter of fact, wanting to spend precious time with him or her is a good sign of how much the couple enjoys each other's company. Spending time with each other away from other responsibilities will strengthen marital bonds.

But… even a simple date gets expensive. It makes a devoted, yet frugally challenged person want to cry. *If you belong to one of those couples without any monetary challenges, feel free to skip this choice. Or, you could consider it a challenge to your dating creativity.*

If we want our marriages to extend a lifetime, we ache for success, but we see this date night idea as a problem. Marriage counselors mean well with the date-night encouragement, but with a little creativity and a lot of persistence other approaches could work too.

What we need is focused time together. We need time to talk and experience life one-on-one. All couples need this to strengthen their connection to one another.

Most of us work separately and reconnect for short stints at the beginning or end of the day, when fatigue takes charge. This left over time cannot and does not strengthen anything.

A date resembles what many people call "quality time." If our busy schedules have us missing each other, a date becomes the quality time we use to reconnect. For years, people have shouted the importance of quality time together, but I've witnessed this piece of fiction in real life.

If you have one friend you visit regularly and another friend who takes you to fancy places once a month. The closest friend is the one who regularly wants to be around you.

The simple truth is this: quantity time trumps quality time every time.

This may make you uncomfortable if you've spent long amounts of time with less than thrilling people, but truth of it is simple. Whatever we do the most will impact us and our marriage the most, whether it's good or bad. So, let's choose to make it good.

In other words, the more time we spend together with our spouse, doing anything, the closer we will be. With that in mind, here are some ways to spend time together, without an official date. Heads up, some of these aren't pretty, but they pack a relational punch.

Cheap Dating Alternatives:

- ❖ Go for a walk or run together. Assuming your kids, if you have them, are old enough to stay home on their own.
- ❖ Play a board game together, while the kids play in another part of the home or after they go to bed.
- ❖ Do yard work together.
- ❖ Read the same book together and share your thoughts.
- ❖ Date at home, once the kids go to bed (if you have younger ones).
- ❖ Delay a nice dinner (just for the two of you) - until after the kids go to bed.
- ❖ Picnic in the living room.
- ❖ Take the laptop or tablet or whatever electronic device you use outside and watch a movie under the stars.
- ❖ His choice (watch his favorite sport or television show together) and talk about it.

- Her choice (watch her favorite cooking show or television show together) and talk about it.
- No Media Monday (or Tues, Wed, whatever). Take one night with no electronic distractions to sit and talk on the couch or at the table about the news of the day or the things that matter to you. Make sure each person gets a chance to share.
- Kid trade. Find other couples with budget issues, and offer to care for one another's kids for free so that each couple gets a chance to be away from the home together and alone.
- Tackle that yucky cleaning job you hate to do, but do it together.
- Open the Bible and read through Song of Songs (or Song of Solomon depending on your translation) together. Get romantically inspired, and laugh your head off at what was considered a compliment in Solomon's day.
- Shop for clothes together. Pick out stuff for the other to try.
- Attend church together.

Make sure to make time for just the two of you. Make it fun, make it real, make it cheap, but be sure to make the time. It matters.

Growth Questions:
- When did you last have a date night of some sort? What made it special? What didn't?

- Look at the list of ideas above. Which one caught your eye?

- Can you think of other ideas you could do together to create an alternative to traditional dating?

Bible verses on this topic:

"What good fellowship we once enjoyed as we walked together to the house of God." Psalm 55:14 (NLT)

"Make every effort to keep yourselves united in the Spirit, binding yourselves together with peace." Ephesians 4:3 (NLT)

"and the two are united into one.' Since they are no longer two but one, let no one split apart what God has joined together." Mark 10:8, 9 (NLT)

"Then make me truly happy by agreeing wholeheartedly with each other, loving one another, and working together with one mind and purpose." Philippians 2:2 (NLT)

Similar choices:

#17 Set Aside Time for Togetherness

#6 Have Fun Together

#8 Hold Hands

12

12. Don't Quit Yet

The hardest day to make a change in life is the first day. In order to succeed, we have to believe it's possible: the dream, the idea, the goal we set is possible. The only way to begin a long hike is to start walking, but most people don't even get to the beginning of the trail. They sit and dream of hiking, but don't even step outside.

In marriage, many of us said we wanted to stay together no matter what, but we didn't know what "no matter what" meant until it arrived at our own doorstep.

Have I mentioned I came from a motivational family? My mom had inspirational recordings playing throughout the house, posters and plaques hung on the walls declaring motivational ideas, some biblical, some just simple encouragement.

They said things like, "God doesn't make junk," "You can soar on the wings of eagles," "Run the race set before you." Maybe they subliminally seeped into my head, but when I get frustrated with life, those images and verses return to me.

And yet, quitting was a constant thought for this girl. It seemed like every time I tried to go beyond my normal boundaries, I felt a push back. I felt incapable of success.

Have you known this feeling?

This foreboding comes upon all of us at one time or another. Steven Pressfield in his book, *The War of Art*, calls this "the resistance." Husbands and wives alike feel the limits of their abilities. We all struggle with what we believe we can or should do. Our nerves get frayed, our tempers roar, our fears build.

The feelings taunt us, daring us to trip and fall or never even try. Those old troubles have messed with us for a while, they know our weaknesses. The feelings convince us of our inabilities, and we quit.

We quit trying to be better or stronger. We buy into that Star Trek line, **"resistance is futile."**

But the truth of life and Star Trek comes in the realization that **resistance is essential.**

Don't get me wrong, if I were writing about how to get a good job, I'd tell you there are times to quit. If I were writing about smoking or drugs or alcohol, I'd shout the value of quitting.

But in living life within our marriages I believe the plaques I read on my walls and many Bible verses grab hands to hold us up. In this place, we must not quit. God has much more for us than we imagine.

When I get exhausted and long to quit anything, I find myself dwelling on one line from a poem I regularly read on my wall. As a teen, I purchased a small card version of the poem, and tucked it into my wallet so I could read it at school.

The poem is entitled, *Don't Quit*. I've placed it here for you to read. My favorite section is emphasized, it's the one I hear in my head when I feel most frustrated. I hope it helps you.

Don't Quit

When things go wrong, as they sometimes will,
When the road you're trudging seems all uphill,
When the funds are low and the debts are high,
And you want to smile, but you have to sigh,

When care is pressing you down a bit,
Rest, if you must, but don't you quit.

Life is queer with its twists and turns,
As every one of us sometimes learns,
And many a failure turns about,
When he might have won had he stuck it out;

Don't give up though the pace seems slow—
You may succeed with another blow.

Often the goal is nearer than,
It seems to a faint and faltering man,

Often the struggler has given up,
When he might have captured the victor's cup,
And he learned too late when the night slipped down,
How close he was to the golden crown.

Success is failure turned inside out–
The silver tint of the clouds of doubt,
And you never can tell how close you are,
It may be near when it seems so far,

So stick to the fight when you're hardest hit–
It's when things seem worst that you must not quit.
- Author anonymous

Success is failure turned inside out. Have you ever thought about this idea? It makes me think of how many times I have messed up before I finally succeeded. It has happened in many parts of my life.

God gives us little peaks of possibility, but we have to believe He will push the clouds away at some point. We will see the sun in its fullness.

Growth Questions:

- What could you be good at in the present, if you hadn't quit in the past? (A sport, playing an instrument, a career skill?)

- Have you ever felt tempted to quit trying to make your marriage stronger? What did you do? Was it helpful?

- When do you feel most tempted to quit? How can you choose to rethink in those moments?

Bible verses on this topic:

"For I can do everything through Christ, who gives me strength." Philippians 4:13 (NLT)

"So, let's not get tired of doing what is good. At just the right time, we will reap a harvest of blessing if we do not give up." Galatians 6:9 (NLT)

Similar choices:

#39 Face the Storms Together

#18 Beware of Joy Zappers

#37 Dream Big

"Kindness is a language which the deaf can hear and the blind can see."
~Mark Twain

Second Gear

We've begun to roll forward on our marital road trip, but we want to travel further and just a bit faster. We push down the clutch and shift into second gear. Now we can move around the neighborhood, past some familiar corners. We may even notice new corners.

13

13. Mind Your Manners

Growing up in a pre-divorce household, my parents barely spoke. When they did, they screamed. They treated one another with disrespectful dissonance, like a wrong chord played at the end of a concert.

For the sake of my brother and me, they made certain deals; who would pick up the kids, who spent time with the kids on weekends.

Since those days, I've witnessed the same in many homes.

Marital struggles can center on finance, on a lack of shared faith, on temptations with food, alcohol, drugs, pornography, etc.

This is yucky deep, down and dirty stuff. If it affects your home, what can you do?

Work on you.

A nagging husband or wife gets nowhere and brings contentment to no one, including themselves. It isn't easy by any means, but it is worth investing the time to work on you rather than only placing responsibility in the lap of your husband or wife.

Many people assume this means counseling, and it can at times. But the first and most valuable place to begin involves growing closer to Christ. When we learn to lean on Him and trust His direction, He helps us learn to think in new ways.

How we think matters.

If the mind always points itself in the direction of trouble, we'll only see the trouble. The Bible refers to the wants we have as human beings as "the flesh." It mentions things we desire, like the stuff found on commercials or images on some Internet sales sites as "fleshly desires."

God makes a big separation between the things of the flesh and the things of the Spirit. He means the difference between stuff we want and stuff God wants for us.

In Romans 8:5-7 (NIV) we read:

"Those who live according to the flesh have <u>their minds set</u> on what the flesh desires; but those who live in accordance with the Spirit have <u>their minds set</u> on what the Spirit desires. <u>The mind</u> governed by the flesh is death, but <u>the mind</u> governed by the Spirit is life and peace. <u>The mind</u> governed by the flesh

is hostile to God; it does not submit to God's law, nor can it do so. Those who are in the realm of the flesh cannot please God."
(I underlined some words to make a point.)

It does little good in our marriage to constantly seek to change your spouse. It's not your job. Regardless of any distress you feel, your job starts with obedience to God. You can seek to control how you think, with His help. As you learn more about Him and His ways, you will grow closer to Him; He enables us all to resist life's temptations.

This resulting closeness brings with it peace and wisdom. It can happen anywhere, even in a tough marriage environment.

How do we learn more about Him and His ways?

1. Read the Bible, God's Word.

If you've never done this before, a wonderful place to start is the book of John. Get an easy to understand Bible like the *New Living Translation*, *New International Version*, or *The Message*. If you have done it before, keep going. This book contains a lifetime of growth possibilities. Its help for us is unlimited. You can even have an app for your phone with the Bible all ready for you to read. My favorite is called the Bible app. (You can find it at www.Bible.com.) If you don't know where to start, I recommend the book of John in the New Testament.

2. Seek out people who have known God longer than you.

If you've ever wondered at the value of attending a church, here it is. Within a church atmosphere, you find people who are living their Christian faith, be it a long or short time. You find support and encouragement for yourself as well as the opportunity to give it. Without supportive people like this, many parts of the Bible are difficult to understand and live.

3. Commit to attending a Christ-Centered Church.

The church may not be perfect, but it still represents the body of Christ. Churches exist for many different personality types: quiet churches, community driven churches, extrovert churches, churches for people who love motorcycles. God provides an assortment to help us.

When they openly declare their faith and what they believe, churches help us to find good learning spaces to grow our faith. You may not be able to attend with your spouse, because of the turmoil you face. This is fine. The goal for now, get your mind right with God.

Then what?

As we grow closer to Christ, He helps us address the issues in marriage that apply to us. He also helps us to face and even appreciate the things in our spouses that seem to cause problems.

God doesn't desire for any of us to get divorced, He longs to see us willingly grow together. With His help and guidance, we can all learn to follow His directions more than our own desires.

Growth Questions:

- Do you ever find yourself looking more at the negative things in marriage than the positive things? What does your mind center on?

- If you're totally honest, what areas could use improvement within your life?

- Have you sought to grow in any of those areas? How can you work on those today?

Bible verses on this topic:

"Stay on the path that the Lord your God has commanded you to follow. Then you will live long and prosperous lives in the land you are about to enter and occupy." Deuteronomy 5:33 (NLT)

"Love the Lord your God with all your heart and with all your soul and with all your mind and with all your strength." Mark 12:30 (NIV)

"Seek the Kingdom of God above all else, and live righteously, and he will give you everything you need." Matthew 6:33 (NLT)

Similar choices:

#52 Make God the Center of Your Marriage

#4 Believe in Change

#16 Follow "The" Role Model

14

14. Laugh at Yourself

Have you ever looked at an old picture of yourself and realized the silliness of the look you were sporting? I have.

In my photo album, my kids often notice my 80's pictures, big hair and all. I wasn't attempting to look clownish with my overly hair-sprayed look, but in retrospect, it was.

No matter how cool we imagine ourselves to be at any given point in time, chances are strong; we'll consider it foolish later.

We might as well be willing to laugh now.

This doesn't mean we should laugh at our husband or wife because they do something foolish. There is a huge difference between laughing at others and laughing at ourselves. The vulnerability of willingly laughing at ourselves helps to bring openness into our relationship.

In an ironic twist, years ago, I learned some of the basics of being a clown. Yes, a real clown. The best clowns encouraged people to laugh at them. The mean ones get people to laugh at someone else.

Inviting the healing nature of laughter into a marriage involves taking the risk of being the source of laughter. When we do it, we become less concerned with ourselves and more open to being generous. Then, something miraculous happens. We become more open, more honest, and more real.

The risk comes when we fear the other person's response. We fear they will grab onto our failures and use them against us. The best way to help a spouse not claim a cause against us is to be sure to not attack them when they get vulnerable.

In the article, *Bringing Laughter into Your Marriage*[ii], for Focus on the Family, Les and Leslie Parrott wrote, "The more you laugh together, the more you love your spouse."

If you keep your eyes open to the giggles around your space, you'll find a joy in marriage that many people long to experience. These giggles come from within and without. The world has so many silly moments we can enjoy together, when we don't take ourselves too seriously.

The photo album is a great place to start seeking giggle moments.

Your sense of humor may not match husband or wife. We each have our own tickle spot, getting to know what brings out a smile in your mate will help you smile too.

Growth Questions:

- What circumstances often bring a burst of laughter from your spouse?

- How can you encourage laughter in each other in a positive way?

- When was the last time you shared a good laugh together?

Bible verses on this topic:

"We were filled with laughter, and we sang for joy. And the other nations said, 'What amazing things the LORD has done for them." Psalm 126:2 (NLT)

"For everything there is a season…a time to cry and a time to laugh, a time to grieve and a time to dance," Ecclesiastes 3:1a and 2 (NLT)

Similar choices:

#11 The Dating Dilemma

#27 Use Words

#6 Have Fun Together

15

15. Serving is Loving

When we receive service at a gas station or a restaurant, another person devotes their energy to fulfilling our needs. Unfortunately, we often associate the word servant with service, not an appealing thought. When did you last meet someone who had the goal of being a servant? We usually think of "service" as menial, low, and lacking value.

If we're being totally honest, we'd rather have a relationship with a husband or wife who serves us. We don't want to serve them or take a low role in the marriage. Like the baboon in a pack who picks fleas off another, we think a servant eats our leftovers or worse.

Did you know Jesus served people?

That's right. The Creator of the universe, God in the flesh, was a flea picker.

As we read the gospels, we witness how He served his disciples by grabbing an apron, some water, and a towel. He cleaned their dirt encrusted feet. He also served all humanity by willingly becoming human to share the everyday struggles we face.

Jesus needed to eat. He required shelter. He had to relieve Himself, if you know what I mean. Jesus probably had a runny nose at some point.

Am I better than Jesus? Are you?

In Gary Chapman's book, *The 5 Love Languages*[iii], he points out how some of us recognize love by how much the other person in our life is willing to serve us. We also give love by serving the person we value.

Jesus proved this valuable lesson by showing his love for us in his servant role. He gave first.

In marriage, our willingness to serve one another is evidence of the love we profess.

Here are some ways we can serve one another:

- Wash the dishes, especially if your husband or wife cooked the meal.
- Claim a dirty job in the house, make it yours by choice: i.e. clean cat litter, take out garbage, etc.
- Bring a lunch to your spouse's work. Drop it and go. Just to show "I love you".
- Serve by giving time and attention.
- Serve by choosing to listen instead of talking.
- Help the kids with homework, especially if it's usually your spouse who does this.
- Make or purchase a meal, if it isn't what you usually do.

- Give your spouse a vacation, let him or her have time to visit with friends or be alone while you stay with the kids or maybe enjoy alone time of your own . (No complaining allowed.)

If it takes energy, effort, and time, and it isn't comfortable, then it's serving.

Growth Questions:

- How do you feel when someone serves you?

- How do you currently serve your spouse? Is this something they want you to do?

- What is a task you could claim as a way of serving your wife or husband?

Bible verses on this topic:

"In your relationships with one another, have the same mindset as Christ Jesus: Who, being in very nature God, did not consider equality with God something to be used to his own advantage; rather, he made himself nothing by taking the very nature of a servant, being made in human likeness. And being found in appearance as a man, he humbled himself by becoming obedient to death— even death on a cross!" Philippians 2:5-8 (NIV)

Similar choices:

#17 Set Aside Time for Togetherness

#7 Walk in Kindness

#29 Let Go of Self

16

16. Follow "The" Role Model

If we want a role model for how to love, it doesn't get better than this. The Bible states in 1 John 4:8,

"God is love." (NIV)

Since God alone possesses perfect DNA, it means He's the best lover of all. In other words, God's the guy to trust on the subject of love. He's the guide, He's the instructor, He's the demonstrator, and He's the meaning itself.

Through the labyrinth of life, we want to walk the proper loving path, but clearly marked directions sometimes allude us. If we believe God is love, we don't assume He'd tease us with unreachable options or fling us into the unknown without a map.

The Bible gives us a definition of love which we can trust God to fulfill. This list of love qualities also provides guidance for those of us who wish to improve our love life. Not only can we read it and find guidance, we can use this description to provide us with steps to improve our love skills.

These verses contain a clear definition of exactly how He thinks of us and what He plans on doing for us. When we live within His strong arms of love, the possibility of us giving it to others opens up, because He guides us step by step and improves on what we thought we knew.

> "Love is patient, love is kind,
> it does not envy, it does not boast,
> it is not proud. It does not dishonor others,
> it is not self-seeking.
> It is not easily angered, it keeps no record of wrongs.
> Love does not delight in evil, but rejoices with the truth.
> It always protects, always trusts, always hopes, always perseveres.
> Love never fails." 1 Corinthians 13:4-8a (NIV)

If you were to separate them one by one, who doesn't want this type of love in their life? I value these verses so much that I used the first part to label my dining room wall. Then, every time I turn my head to yell or respond to someone else down my hallway, my eyes first notice the words, "Love is patient, love is kind."

These are not quick and simple things to discover and refine in our homes. Every sentence, every pause between the commas takes time. As you continue to read the choices found within this book many of them came from a desire to follow the example set forth in this group of verses.

When these verses get taken together the choices might overwhelm us with a sense of responsibility, and we become frustrated by our lack of skill. That's okay. No one except God does this all perfectly. But, we can improve.

If we trust in the One who made all this love stuff in the first place, we'll discover our love life has improved in ways we never expected.

Take a moment and reread 1 Corinthians 13: 4-8a. Consider which of these expressions of love you most want to witness in your marriage and share it with your spouse. Then, consider which of these love expressions you would most like to improve, remembering we can only improve ourselves.

Growth Questions:
- What expression of love do you understand best in God?

- How can you use Him as a role model within your marriage?

- When you read the verses on love, which elements do you find most important?

Bible verses on this topic:
"God is love." 1 John 4:8 (NIV)

"Love is patient, love is kind, it does not envy, it does not boast, it is not proud. It does not dishonor others, it is not self-seeking. It is not easily angered, it keeps no record of wrongs. Love does not delight in evil, but rejoices with the truth. It always protects, always trusts, always hopes, always perseveres. Love never fails." 1 Corinthians 13:4-8a (NIV)

Similar choices:
#52 Make God the Center of Your Marriage
#4 Believe in Change
#22 Sit on the Chair

17

17. Set Aside Time for Togetherness

We want, love, and need time: time with others, time to think, time to work, time to play. This valuable commodity tells us and others what we value. Unlike money, it is a nonrenewable resource. Once a day has passed, we cannot get it back. Therefore, how we use our time indicates what we value. With our busy lives, how much time do we give to our husband or wife?

Because of our different life lenses, we may or may not receive love the same way. For example, I am big on time.

I believe people care for me when they make an effort to spend time with me. If asked about my favorite birthday experience, it would have to be my 25th birthday, because my friends and family invested time in their gift.

My mother called people she didn't know to invite them to a meal at one of my favorite restaurants. She invited me to join her for dinner and surprised me with the thirty plus people who came. There was more.

A close friend created my own personal scavenger hunt. It began at the restaurant and ended at our shared apartment. She created clues and took me all over town.

She involved several mutual friends. Those two entirely separate experiences given on one night made it my best birthday celebration ever.

Why?

They took time to call, to set things up, to write clues and to have people stationed in various locations. These things told my time-impressed brain, "They really care."

In our marriages, how often do we take the time to be together to show how much we appreciate each other? For those of us who really understand love through the lens of time, this one plucks our heart strings.

Ways to use time to show love:

- **Pause in your day to call or text your spouse** and tell them you value them. A "time" person knows the effort you made.

- **Turn off the TV or computer.** Sit with your husband or wife. Ask about their day. Share about your day too. This time cannot be replaced.

- **Plan to purposely meet for lunch on a work day**. Rather than networking with work people, get together with the person you love most.

- **Mark the calendar and set aside at least one hour a week with your husband or wife.** Whether you do a stay-at-home date or go out, make it a sacred time in your week. When you receive other invitations, don't let this one get touched. It matters.

- **Make a plan and discuss what you each enjoy doing with your time** (sports, TV, talking, walking, eating, etc.). Rotate sharing those experiences together balancing what each of you love to do.

- **Do chores together.** They go faster, and you grow because of it. Cleaning the dishes becomes a blessing rather than a burden.

Growth Questions:

- Time is a valuable commodity, since it cannot be replaced. Think of a moment when someone gave of their time to help or give to you. How did it make you feel?

- In what ways do you currently give your time to show your love for your husband or wife?

- Could you do more? What could you do tomorrow to use time as an expression of love?

Bible verses on this topic:

"I thank my God every time I remember you." Philippians 1:3 (NIV)

"Because we loved you so much, we were delighted to share with you not only the gospel of God but our lives as well." 1 Thessalonians 2:8 (NIV)

Similar choices:

#3 Be Present

#11 The Dating Dilemma

#33 Practice Patience

18

18. Beware of Joy Zappers

Have you ever played the wet towel game?

Pick up a slightly wet towel, twirl it until it's twisted tightly, and then zap some unsuspecting person by whipping it quickly at them with one hand. If you've been on the receiving end, you know the stinging feeling.

The game seems fun until someone makes contact, and then revenge takes over. The target now aims all his efforts toward making the attacker feel the same pain.

Certain situations or people in our life become joy zappers. They make a snap connection and bring out a desire within us to impose trouble on others rather than joy. It happens so fast we don't always realize it until we've been zapped.

Those zappers do have a habit of smacking others. Like the one person in our family most likely to twist up a towel while washing the car, we need to keep a wary eye out for joy zappers.

As a child, my zapper was my brother. Literally, he'd zap me with a towel any chance he could. Other things and people zap us once we become adults. Having an open eye and wary attitude will keep us prepared. Our marriages also need to be guarded against life's joy zappers.

The Zap List:

News Channels

It's helpful to be aware of needs within our community, but news channels feed on the pain of others. My husband often describes the helicopters gathering above an accident on the freeway as flies around dung. I wish they could make good money by telling us the great things people do every day, but unfortunately it doesn't work that way. Pain and destruction are their bread and butter. Watch and beware.

Well-meaning friends

We all have these people in our lives, the ones who only bring bad news to the party. They rarely say a positive word. They often speak with authority about things they don't know.

Remember to consider the source

The friend with three divorces doesn't have good marriage advice to share. The friend with tornado teenagers can't help with parenting guidance. The friend who has tons of debt won't increase our monetary wisdom.

The book of Job shows how helpful this sort of friend can be. Job's world crumbled around him through no fault of his own and three "friends" spent quality time telling him to confess his sins and hate God. It's happened since the beginning of time, and it continues today.

Negative Self-Talk

Sometimes we don't need anyone else to bring yuck into our lives. Between our own insecurities and any previous negative comment made to us throughout our entire lives, we become our own joy zapper. The thoughts start small, then, we feed them by continuing to think and dwell on them. The snowball of all zaps begins to roll down our virtual hill. This one can smack us like no other because only we can stop it. How? Bring in outside help.

Finding Help

Ask God to help you think another way. Ask God to remove these thoughts, to shut them down. Ask God to give you positive thoughts and ideas. Here's a place to start:

"I praise you because I am fearfully and wonderfully made; your works are wonderful, I know that full well." Psalm 139:14 (NIV)

Statistics have shown that we all require at least five positive comments to overcome one negative, we can choose to do the same with our self-talk, or the negatives others sling our way by telling ourselves positive things rather than negative.

Our marriages encounter joy zappers every day. People who want us to think of spouses as drains on our energy. News stories repeatedly show how uncaring people can be toward one another. Our own personal history makes us doubt the love of our spouse.

The more time we spend seeking to learn what God thinks, the stronger our joy becomes. His perspective always brings hope and encouragement even in the toughest times of life.

Growth Questions:

- What joy zappers do you have in your life?

- How can you seek to avoid the joy zappers?

- How do you plan to spend more time seeking God's direction in your life?

Bible verses on this topic:

"Splendor and majesty are before him; strength and joy are in his dwelling place." 1 Chronicles 16:27 (NIV)

"I have told you these things so that you will be filled with my joy. Yes, your joy will overflow!" John 15:11 (NLT)

"The precepts of the LORD are right, giving joy to the heart. The commands of the LORD are radiant, giving light to the eyes." Psalm 19:8 (NIV)

Similar choices:

#26 Face Your Fears

#39 Face the Storms Together

#36 Spend Well

19

19. Support One Another, Especially When It's Tough

Have you ever woken up to the feeling of fever wrapping itself around your body? It deflates your energy and desire, you feel trapped.

It's also one of the greatest marriage-making moments.

We hope for trips to Disney or the beach, but illness shows the strength within a marriage. It also exposes weaknesses. Marriages prove themselves in the tough times. Whether your marriage proves itself through a slow crawl or a mighty roar, it still proves itself.

Marriages get hit by nastiness every day.

Financial challenges, communication weaknesses, illness and more cause us to lean on one another or pull away.

When a husband prepares dinner after a long day at work or wife shaves her head to show a commitment to a husband beginning radiation therapy, marriage muscles form that strengthen the couple in amazing ways.

Marriage is not about vacations. It's not about buying the best car or house. Marriage matters because of the support we give and receive when times get tough, even if tough happens all the time.

My grandmother discovered she had a severe form of rheumatoid arthritis in her early twenties. The doctors told her to lie down and stay down. They believed rest would help.

Suddenly, my grandfather found himself needing to make the meals and clean the home, while he continued working as a mortgage broker. In his time, these jobs were considered "woman's work." This trial showed them both the depth of his love.

The man made some pretty good chicken soup.

Growth Questions:

- How do you behave when you face financial or health difficulties?

- How would you change your attitude if you considered the strength provided by enduring these difficulties?

- Think of a time you grew stronger because of a difficult situation. What can you do to recall this moment when tough stuff hits your marriage?

Bible verses on this topic:

"You, my brothers and sisters, were called to be free. But do not use your freedom to indulge the flesh; rather, serve one another humbly in love." Galatians 5:13 (NIV)

"Be devoted to one another in love. Honor one another above yourselves." Romans 12:10 (NIV)

Similar choices:

#17 Set Aside Time for Togetherness

#39 Face the Storms Together

#25 Pack Some Gear, Expect a Long Ride

20

20. Give a Shout Out

Jarod often complains at work about his wife Lena: she doesn't cook, she doesn't clean, and she doesn't do anything for him. He tells his colleagues repeatedly about how she only cares about herself. After a while of hearing his complaints, his colleagues find it difficult to understand why they married in the first place.

Like Jarod, many of us have adopted a habit of complaining about our lives. We complain about our spouse more often than we praise. We ridicule them in front of their peers and our friends.

As a result, an underlying feeling of anger and resentment builds in our marriage until someone doesn't want to stick around to hear it anymore.

But what if…

We chose to seek opportunities to praise our loved ones. Because of our love for them, we don't cover over problems; instead, we search for blessings. Those blessings become the things we tell others about our spouse. As we share the pluses, we notice them more. They feel our love through our words and our attitudes.

The more we declare praise for those we love, the more we believe it and the less we resent them for other failings. After all, they are human and therefore not perfect. Imagine if this were done for you.

Growth Questions:

- Do you complain about your spouse to other people in your life? Why or why not?

- What characteristics about your spouse are worth praising?

- How can you begin to praise your spouse to other people in your life?

Bible verses on this topic:

"Out of the same mouth come praise and cursing. My brothers and sisters, this should not be." James 3:10 (NIV)

"We work wearily with our own hands to earn our living. We bless those who curse us. We are patient with those who abuse us." 1 Corinthians 4:12 (NLT)

Similar choices:

#19 Support One Another, Especially When It's Tough

#10 Tame the Tongue

#43 Count the Pluses

21

21. Be a Gift Giver

James has been married for 10 years with one main frustration. His wife never gives him gifts, never.

She never gives him a birthday present, and she never makes him a meal. There are other pluses in their marriage, but gifts matter to him. She doesn't know it.

For some people receiving a gift helps them recognize love. These gifts take many shapes. We can keep our eyes open for the gift that suits our spouse. Giving the kind of gifts we'd like to receive may not help; our spouses may not want the same things we want.

I'll never forget the year I gave my husband, Tim, a camera for Christmas, because I wanted more family photos. To justify the gift, I told myself how much he enjoys photography, which is true. He takes good pictures, so I gave him the camera.

He used the camera once or twice, but thereafter I took charge of it. I encouraged him to bring it on trips, but I took the pictures. On reflection, I bought the camera for myself.

Men do the same when they buy their wives lingerie. From the woman's point of view, it isn't comfortable; we aren't attempting to make ourselves feel sexy. Except for a brief glance in the mirror, we don't look at ourselves in it. When a husband purchases this gift for his wife, he really wants to please himself. However, if a wife purchases the lingerie because she knows it will please her husband, it's a gift for him.

For any gift to be an expression of love, it must take into account what the receiver most wants. A gift well given shows how well the giver listened to the needs and desires of the receiver.

To test if your spouse sees gifts as an expression of love, you need to ask.

What would he or she rather have you do: speak great words, give a gift, do a project, help in a practical way or something else? A straight forward question opens doors of insight. If he doesn't know how to respond, test him by giving him a gift. Do his eyes light up? Then, he likes gifts.

If gift-giving clicks for your loved one, check out the list below.

Tips for successful gift giving:

Ask questions to discover what the receiver wants.

For example, instead of asking, "What do you want?" ask "What did you do today?" In response to "What did you do?" you can ask, "What did you wish you could do?" This little question can inspire gifts that demonstrate how well you listen and care.

Discover a favorite gift from the past.

Knowing what gifts have touched the receiver's heart previously will help with the future. Seeking to learn why a gift meant a great deal will determine if you could give such a gift or not.

Talk to other close friends

To determine a good gift more voices bring more choices.

Think through the gift.

Seek to determine if it will bring joy to the heart of the person you love.

A good gift can be cheap, fun, or exciting. It can be different from flowers, chocolate, dinner or a movie. Great gift giving requires thought and preparation for it to truly delight the one you love. It will demonstrate love in a practical way.

If you are one who enjoys receiving gifts, make sure to express your thanks. A little encouragement helps in a huge way, especially if the giver is trying to do something new.

Jesus gave us the best gift when He came to live among us, die for us, stick around, and rise for us. He was the gift. His gift demonstrated the depths He goes to prove His love.

God's gift-giving ability exceeds our ability, but He also sets a standard for us to follow. A well thought out gift shows love.

Growth Questions:

- What is the best gift you ever received? Think about why it was the best.

- What is the best gift you ever gave? Was it the best because of how it made you feel or how the receiver responded?

- How can you improve on your gift-giving skills?

Bible verses on this topic:

"Every good and perfect gift is from above, coming down from the Father of the heavenly lights, who does not change like shifting shadows."
James 1:17 (NIV)

"Giving a gift can open doors; it gives access to important people!"
Proverbs 18:16 (NLT)

Similar choices:

#11 The Dating Dilemma

#9 Bank on Marriage

#7 Walk in Kindness

22

22. Sit on the Chair

Every day we show how much we trust a builder we've never met. When we get up in the morning and sit at the table for breakfast, we assume the chair will hold our bodies securely.

I know this is true, because I built several chairs for my church when we moved to a new building. They came with instructions and needed to be attached with screws, nuts, and bolts.

I followed the directions and used a screw driver to secure legs and seats. They felt good to me. But, I underestimated the use they would receive. My muscles couldn't secure the screws as tightly as they required. As hundreds of people came into the room with those chairs in the following days, I noticed something disturbing.

Chairs started moving to the side of the room and required repair. When I investigated further, I saw the problem. The screws were coming loose.

The builder, me, hadn't fastened them tight enough. In the weeks following, a generous man with a drill driver used his power tool to improve the job I had done with good intentions.

The people who sat on my chairs believed I had prepared the chair properly and many had chairs fall apart beneath them because of my weak skills. If we regularly place trust in builders we never met, shouldn't we extend this same grace and trust to the people who have committed to spend a lifetime with us?

Real love involves sitting in our relationship chair and expecting it to hold us. It also means our precious loved ones should expect the same from us. Because of our failing muscles, we also need to recognize the imperfect skills of our beloved.

It's time to trust and become someone our spouse can trust in return.

Growth Questions:

- When was the last time you felt as if your spouse let you down?

- When did you let them down?

- How can you decide to trust your spouse, in spite of imperfections, ecause you know your own failings too?

A Bible verse on this topic:

"Dear children, let's not merely say that we love each other; let us show the truth by our actions." 1 John 3:18 (NLV)

"A wicked messenger falls into trouble, but a trustworthy envoy brings healing." Proverbs 13:17 (NIV)

Similar choices:

#19 Support One Another, Especially When It's Tough

#4 Believe in Change

#50 Be the Good Wife

#51 Be the Good Husband

23

23. Take Sage Advice

Do you know any couples who have been married 20, 30, 40 or more years? What does their marriage look like?

I've had the privilege of knowing many amazing couples. Not perfect couples, but amazing none the less. When asked about their relationship you can see the pleasure or displeasure in their eyes.

Recently, I assessed how many couples I know who have been married a long time, couples who truly enjoy spending time together and would do it again in an instant. Do you know people like this?

What a great resource they provide! They generously give a visual example of how they do the long-term thing. Their willingness to share their stories, both good and bad helps those of us with younger marriages to picture something more. It's the kind of knowledge you can only gain from first-hand experience.

CNN and Time Magazine shared a video of a couple from Las Vegas who have been married for 80 years[iv]. They are believed to be the "Longest Married Couple." To hear Wilber, the husband, talk, they are still in love.

We can infer further proof of the solidity of their marriage because their son entered their information into this contest to discover the longest married couple.

Just hearing about their longevity makes my little wedding ring finger wiggle with joy. It's encouraging and instructive. How wonderful to get to see it and therefore believe it.

Couples like this make me want to say, "Teach me, Obi wan." (That's a Star Wars reference for you non-fans.)

Reporters sharing this story felt the same way I did; they needed to know how the couple did it. Wilber described the secret to their long marriage saying, "It's simple. It's give and take and compromise."

Seeing people like this couple provides inspiration for us to stick with marriage, no matter what happens. If you don't know any long-term marriages that you respect, it's time to start looking and asking advice.

Growth Questions:

- Think of people you know who have been married for 20, 30, 40 or more years. Do you believe they have a good marriage?

- If you don't know anyone with a long-term marriage, where could you look to find these couples?

- What questions could you ask to get coaching from those who have been married longer than you?

Bible verses on this topic:

"Love prospers when a fault is forgiven, but dwelling on it separates close friends." Proverbs 17:9 (NLT)

"Do two walk together unless they have agreed to do so?" Amos 3:3 (NIV)

"Finally, all of you, be like-minded, be sympathetic, love one another, be compassionate and humble." 1 Peter 3:8 (NIV)

Similar choices:

#5 Hang Out with Inspiring Couples

#1 Seek Sticky Truths

#25 Pack Some Gear, Expect a Long Ride

24

24. Married Not Buried

I remember the day I discovered my grandpa noticed girls. At approximately 75 years of age, I thought those ideas had left his brain. Clearly, I was wrong.

He and my grandma had an amazing marriage. Of this, I have no doubt. Grandma had rheumatoid arthritis and her 4 foot 11 body had crumpled from the disease. Her joints had been removed in her fingers and toes due to the intensity of the pain. She used a wheel chair every day.

Grandpa cared for her in every possible way. He learned to cook to feed their family at a time when husbands didn't do the cooking. At the age of 28, my grandma had been told to remain in bed. At first she just needed crutches, but eventually a wheelchair became her only method of movement.

He took her places in her wheel chair, they talked about everything. She had a special beauty to her countenance, and he showed his appreciation and adoration for her regularly.

When I think of kindness within marriage, I picture my grandpa.

It never occurred to me that Grandpa would ever look at another woman. They had been married 45 years at the time. And yet he did.

Our family went to a local Marriott in Phoenix, Arizona for a meal. The restaurant was a favorite of my grandma. Following the meal we wandered about the resort and stopped to talk near the swimming pool. Grandma loved the different types of pools found at Arizona resorts.

As we stood, a few feet from a waterfall, one of the poolside attendants strolled past us carrying a tray of food. In mid-conversation, my grandpa paused and gazed in her direction, his head turned to follow her as she delivered the snack to a guest. She wore a one-piece, backless, red bathing suit.

As you can imagine, Grandpa noticed the backless part as she passed us.

In that moment, I realized he was married, not buried.

He passionately loved my grandma and held back no affection from her, yet his eyes noticed beauty when it crossed his path. However, I saw something else too. His eyes didn't linger.

Do you know what I mean, linger?

He caught himself and mentally returned to be fully present with Grandma. My incredibly wise grandma said, "Oh Johnny," and laughed at his obvious observation. She confidently knew his true affections remained with her.

This stood in opposition to something I witnessed from my dad.

My parents' marriage struggled for multiple reasons, not the least involved my dad's view of women. He treated women as objects to be ogled, not people to be appreciated.

How do I know?

My father kept a separate apartment from our home. I regularly visited him there. On the bathroom wall, across from the toilet, he and his business partner had posted a page from Playboy Magazine. It was exactly as bad as you imagine. I cannot begin to explain the depth of humiliation and attack I felt when I regularly saw this picture. I was eight years old at the time.

The idea of growing up with a man as my male role model who saw that as my place in society made me want to vomit.

As a young woman being raised with these two distinctly different men, I learned to appreciate the eyes that notice beauty but don't linger or ogle.

"Love is kind..." 1 Corinthians 13:4 (NIV)

Pornography kills marriages just as much as money or affairs. It brings with it a lack of caring and kindness for the women being ogled. It desensitizes us to genuine connection of heart and mind.

Men or women who submerse themselves in pornography carry into their lives a lack of respect for other people and for reality. (We've all heard of Photoshop, right? That's what I mean when I mention a lack of respect for reality.)

Pastor and Blogger Jonathan Pearson wrote an blogpost[v] quoting a CNN Health[vi] article on the results of pornography and video game playing. In the article by Dr. Philip G. Zimbardo and Nikita Duncan, CNN stated, "The excessive use of video games and online porn in pursuit of the next thing is creating a generation of risk-averse guys who are unable (and unwilling) to navigate the complexities and risks inherent to real-life relationships, school and employment."

Jonathan Pearson responded referring to those who take it to extremes, "After all, if we pretend enough, we begin to convince ourselves it's reality."

From the woman's point of view, we often get caught up in novels designed to entice and stimulate. Though many women do watch pornography (*which damages us too*), these novels bring the same result. We begin to expect something unrealistic of the men in our lives. Our minds think of how great it would be to have a caring male figure like the perfect ones in these books. Or perhaps one who sweeps us off our feet.

In the same way, we women ogle the men. We let our minds linger on what it would be like to have such a man in our lives, an equally destructive idea no real man can match.

In an article on her website *Girls Gone Wise*[vii], Mary Kassian wrote about the erotic novel *Fifty Shades of Grey*, which many women have read; Amazon lists it in the top ten of Women's Fiction.

She says, "The problem with erotica, as with porn, is that you'll end up craving increasingly graphic, perverse images over time. Erotica/porn leads to deeper, darker erotica/porn. What's more, they end up robbing people of the joy and satisfaction of "ordinary," non-twisted sex with an "ordinary" spouse."

When we open the door of our hearts to pornography whether written or visual, it entraps us and keeps us from extending kindness to those we love.

Growth Questions:

- Have you felt yourself tempted to ogle someone? When? What did you do?

- Have you ever felt ogled? How did you respond?

- What can you do to resist the temptation to let your eyes or mind linger where it will not please God?

Bible verses on this topic:

"I keep my eyes always on the LORD. With him at my right hand, I will not be shaken." Psalm 16:8 (NIV)

"Above all else, guard your heart, for everything you do flows from it." Proverbs 4:23 (NIV)

Similar choices:

#1 Seek Sticky Truths

#43 Count the Pluses

#49 Learn the Secret

"For everything that was written in the past
was written to teach us,
so that through the endurance taught in the Scriptures
and the encouragement they provide
we might have hope."
Romans 15:4

Third Gear

You're clearly a driver, and you're moving forward. It's time to leave your comfortable neighborhood to venture into the rest of town. You'll encounter many corners, but I'll bet you can handle it. Though, it may take practice to build comfort.

25

25. Pack Some Gear, Expect a Long Ride

When we hit the road, we bring with us those things we feel we'll need for the trip we planned. A picnic needs plates, cups and food. An overnight camping trip at Yosemite requires a bit more. A year in France means a bigger commitment to planning.

How long do you expect your marriage to last?

Micah couldn't imagine living without his wife Danielle. She, however, figured he'd get tired of her. She thought he'd want to move on one day. Because she assumed he would leave, she told herself it wouldn't last. From the day they got married, she pictured a short relationship.

Henry Ward Beecher said, "The difference between perseverance and obstinacy is that one often comes from a strong will, and the other from a strong won't."

Micah believed in marriage. In his mind, he thought, "I will live with her forever."

Danielle doubted the level of his love. She convinced herself the marriage wouldn't last. She told herself, "It won't continue."

Many of us get married with the idea of leaving if it doesn't work well. Only when we decide the exit isn't an option do we really begin to open ourselves up for all the possibilities love has for us. When those around us know we plan on staying, they will respond accordingly, as long as they plan on sticking around too.

This isn't the end of the story for Micah and Danielle. If you've felt similar feelings, it isn't the end of the story for you either. Like resetting the GPS in our car for a new destination, we can decide we want a longer trip.

Growth Questions:

- Right now, how long do you believe your relationship will last?

- In what way does your activity in marriage reflect this thought process?

- What can you do to begin or continue thinking long term rather than short term?

Bible verses on this topic:

"Blessed is the one who perseveres under trial because, having stood the test, that person will receive the crown of life that the Lord has promised to those who love him." James 1:12 (NIV)

"For you know that when your faith is tested, your endurance has a chance to grow." James 1:3 (NLT)

Similar choices:

#5 Hang Out with Inspiring Couples

#1 Seek Sticky Truths

#24 Married Not Buried

26

26. Face Your Fears

During our first year of marriage, I recall a conversation with my new husband that struck a tender chord in my heart. As he fell asleep, my mind kept churning; I analyzed and reanalyzed each word he had said. It's fair to say I obsessed. Eventually, I found myself curled up in a corner of our home convulsing with tears.

What had he said? To this day, I don't remember. What I do recall is the fear within me. It wrapped itself around my heart and told me, "I can't do this. I can't be the kind of wife people talk about. I don't want to be the kind of wife I pictured in old books and fairy tales."

Fear gripped my being in a fury of insecurity like an animal clawing at me from within.

We all feel fear at some point. Don't we?

Even the famous singer, Taylor Swift said, "I'm intimidated by the fear of being average."

Whatever issue attacks your heart, many people have spoken on the topic of fear. Want more words of wisdom?

- There is a time to take counsel of your fears, and there is a time to never listen to any fear.
  ~George S. Patton (World War II General)

- I have learned over the years that when one's mind is made up, this diminishes fear.
  ~Rosa Parks (Civil rights initiator)

- The way you overcome shyness is to become so wrapped up in something that you forget to be afraid.
  ~Lady Bird Johnson (First Lady of the United States)

- The greatest mistake we make is living in constant fear that we will make one.
  ~John C. Maxwell (author, speaker, trainer of leaders)

I read a book that addresses fear in a raw manner. It's called *The Flinch*[viii], by Julien Smith. Amazon sells the eBook for free, and it is worth so much more. This book details the process people undergo to silence their instinct to flinch when faced with difficulties of some sort. I loved the practical application moments when it guides the readers to do various tasks that many people fear.

I learned more than I could have imagined by completing a task where Julien asks his reader to take a cold shower for 15 minutes. As a California born and Arizona bred heat lover, I despised the idea of it, but I did it. On my blog, I wrote an article entitled, *Fear and the Cold Shower*, about the experience I had and how it has helped with some fears I have.

Julien gives great advice for those who long to move forward and not flinch. But if I'm going to trust anyone, it will be God first. We can kneel—yes, I said kneel—before God and ask for His help in facing our fears.

He has promised never to leave us. We can disclose our darkest, goose bump giving terrors to Him. Not only does He still like us and believe in us, He enables us to push through even the toughest relational fear.

It also helps to confess our fear to those we love and ask them to pray with us on the issues that torture us most. If your spouse isn't the one to trust, find a friend who has a strong and long lived marriage to share your struggle. Make sure this person also trusts God for direction. Ask them to pray with you. You can even ask God to help your spouse to become more trustworthy.

Growth Questions:

- What causes you to feel goose bump giving terror within your relationship?

- What have you normally done when the fear strikes? Ask God to give you an alternative direction.

- How can you give yourself a reminder to take the fear to God first rather than dwelling on it?

Bible verses on this topic:

"For God has not given us a spirit of fear and timidity, but of power, love and self-discipline." 2 Timothy 1:7 (NLT)

"I sought the LORD, and he answered me; he delivered me from all my fears." Psalm 34:4 (NIV)

"Cast your cares on the LORD and he will sustain you; he will never let the righteous be shaken." Psalm 55:22 (NIV)

Similar choices:

#12 Don't Quit Yet

#18 Beware of Joy Zappers

#49 Learn the Secret

27

27. Use Words

At the core of any relationship we find communication. What we say and how we say it matters.

Do you remember the good old days when only guys felt as if they didn't understand women? If we're completely honest ladies, we don't always understand men either. If we did, our divorce rate wouldn't be skyrocketing. After all, it takes at least two to toss the minivan in a lake.

Anika never said a kind word to Royce. She used sarcasm as her love tool. At first, Royce found it cute. They verbally spared as the romance built. Fast forward ten years, Royce lost his job. He spent all day hunting for a new one. Anika knew he worked hard, she believed he could do anything he tried. But, out her mouth came another message.

With the feelings of stress already present and the insecurity brought on by job loss, Royce's sense of humor got buried deep in their backyard. He couldn't handle hearing one more negative word. He walked away from their relationship.

How we communicate will either grow our relationship or tear it apart. For some people, properly expressed words connect with their hearts in an almost magical way. A switch gets turned; they see the level of caring because of the words spoken, if those words are spoken wisely.

Couples discover roadblocks to this area in their marriage all the time. It's easy to complain to other people about problems at home without ever addressing them directly.

Consider Royce. He complained to his friends about Anika's lack of caring for years. But, except for the occasional yelling fest, he never really spoke with her.

Why?

Many couples do the same. They risk the same result.

The less we connect with each other verbally, the less we understand one another. In spite of the many movies that place an emphasis on some sort of nonverbal relationship insight, most of us cannot read minds. We make assumptions about the other based on our own way of thinking.

If we assume we have a strong nonverbal connection, we think we know answers to questions we've never asked. Real communication requires both speaking and listening.

Couples who take the time to listen, who risk sharing real feelings with one another, will communicate successfully. For this to happen, we must choose to be the first to ask questions.

A friend of mine likes to say, "We were given two ears and one mouth as evidence of which should be used more."

Imagine what might have happened if Royce had told Anika how she made him feel with her sarcastic barbs. What if Anika had asked Royce how she could support him?

Questions help us to continually grow closer regardless of changes happening in and around us. Good questions encourage an answer other than the non-communicative "yes," "no," or "fine." Without effort, our communication goes no further than a short grunt.

Question suggestions:

1. What was something funny that happened to you today?
2. How can I help you?
3. What news have you heard today? What did you think about it?
4. Did you have any good discussions today? What were they about?
5. What was your favorite part of the day? Why?
6. Were there any bad parts to your day? What happened?

These six questions won't fit every situation, but they can inspire us to develop our own questions. Remember, we're choosing to be the conversation starter, not the topic.

Learning to communicate in this way requires patience, but it's worth the effort.

Growth Questions:

- What types of discussions do you and your spouse usually have?

- Can you think of something you've held onto and not shared with your spouse? What's keeping you from sharing it?

- Think of questions to ask him or her today. What are they?

Bible verses on this topic:

"Words from the mouth of the wise are gracious, but fools are consumed by their own lips." Ecclesiastes 10:12 (NIV)

"Wise words bring many benefits, and hard work brings rewards." Proverbs 12:14 (NLV)

"Some people make cutting remarks, but the words of the wise bring healing." Proverbs 12:18 (NLV)

Similar choices:

#31 Communicate Generously

#41 Listen Up

#46 Back off Boasting Words

28

28. Try, Try Again... In the Bedroom

I have no illusions of profound wisdom when it comes to sex, but I know what I've lived; the conversations I've had. Through open honesty with friends and my husband, I learned a profound lesson early on which I want to pass to you.

In my twenties, I helped teens come to know the Lord at a Young Life camp one summer. Much effort and time went into communicating the gospel in a loving, sincere way. The camp wanted to address real issues teens face. I'll never forget one of the speakers who did a round table discussion on the topic of sex.

He talked about being faithful to one another. He shared his insight on God's design for keeping a commitment in relationships. He answered many teen questions about sex. One question in particular stuck with me.

A teenage boy asked, "Isn't it better to live together; to try and see if you're sexually compatible?"

At the time, I was single. I knew people who lived together. I researched the longevity comparison between couples who live together and those in a committed marriage. Statistically speaking, living together doesn't pay off for the long term. And yet it somehow sounds like it will.

Sitting in the room packed with teens and helpful adults, you could hear people blink as they anxiously awaited his answer.

He said, "Me and my wife have a simple approach which works well for us. If at first you don't succeed, try, try again."

I laughed at the irony of his statement, but those 9 words remained stuck in my head. In my own marriage, I have since learned what great advice it is.

Movies or videos give us a false idea of sexual romance. Keep in mind, each image is directed, choreographed, practiced, filmed and redone until it fits the genre it's meant to portray. Real life doesn't work in the same way.

We adopt a culture of self-centeredness concerning sex when we assume that each time should be the "best time" of our lives. What pressure we place on ourselves and our loved ones!

Real people deal with kids, pets, outside noises, personal stress and so on. We require a relationship where forgiveness and adaptability applies. And, if you can laugh, that's much better.

Growth Questions:

- What did you think sex would be like when you got married?

- How has the reality of marriage altered that image?

- Does your spouse matter enough for you to be willing to try, try again with a forgiving and adaptable attitude? What can you do to adopt this attitude?

Bible verses on this topic:

"But if we look forward to something we don't yet have, we must wait patiently and confidently." Romans 8:25 (NLT)

"Be completely humble and gentle; be patient, bearing with one another in love." Ephesians 4:2 (NIV)

Similar choices:

#17 Set Aside Time for Togetherness

#45 Forgive Often

#8 Hold Hands

29

29. Let Go of Self

We long for more loving relationships for ourselves, but love isn't all about us. Genuine love dreams the best for the other person. This presents a confusing conundrum.

Jonah wants his wife, Elaine, to spend more time with him. She works constantly, driving their three kids from event or club after event or club, while she also picks up some cash as a hair stylist. As an airline pilot, he assumes she should spend every bit of his home time with him. Meanwhile, Elaine wishes him would trade and become the taxi driver when he returns home.

We all feel their pain, and yet we all see the problem. In order for success in their marriage someone's got to give.

We express love, when we give without expecting something in return. God shows His love for us this way. He gave the biggest sacrifice, His Son, before we even knew how much He loved us. He did it knowing how many people would still reject His gift.

Because God gave so freely, we become enabled to give too.

We believe our husband or wife loves us, because of their generosity toward us. We also prove we love, because we give without focusing on ourselves.

It has to start with someone, why not you?

Growth Questions:

- Have you ever felt like Jonah or Elaine? What did you do about it?

- When do you feel most tempted to focus on your own needs within your marriage?

- What is one way you could reach out today and give to your spouse unconditionally? (Notice I mentioned the spouse not the kids, we get trained in giving unconditionally to the kids. It takes effort to give to our spouse.)

Bible verses on this topic:

"For you have been called to live in freedom, my brothers and sisters. But don't use your freedom to satisfy your sinful nature. Instead, use your freedom to serve one another in love." Galatians 5:13 (NLV)

"Freely you have received; freely give." Matthew 10:8b (NIV)

Similar choices:

#2 Think Like a Team

#17 Set Aside Time for Togetherness

#31 Communicate Generously

#35 Devote Yourself to the Essentials

30

30. Record and Remember the Good

We all have a check list in our heads. When the people we love impress us, we check the good side. When we feel as if they fail us, we check the bad side.

Have you ever noticed how we open our mouths for commentary more often when the bad side gets checked?

It makes me think of Sam and Edna. Edna had a habit of telling Sam about his past mistakes whenever he made a present mistake. She said things like, "You always forget my birthday," or "You never listen to my opinions."

The same thing happens to many of us. We don't just mention a current bad moment, like forgetting to take out the trash or balance the check book, we run down the list of all the previous bad moments as if we're Santa reading the naughty list. Something could have happened years ago, but once we get going on that bad side, watch out.

WARNING! This is a trap!

If we look at the person we love from the bad side of the list, we won't love them very long. Everyone has a bad side, including us. If we seek to focus on the good, the more good we say about them, the better we see them. Then, they respond to our positive words.

How do you react when someone says something good about you?

Praise in the office place creates a better worker; the same can be said for the home. Our loved ones become better when we regularly notice and appreciate their strengths. It works! (*But it will take time to seep in, if we've previously spent time pointing toward the bad side.*)

Growth Questions:

- What type of comments do you make the most, the positive ones or the negative ones?

- How do you respond when your spouse or someone close points to your negative side?

- What good points can you remember to focus on when making comments about or to your spouse?

Bible verses on this topic:

"Be devoted to one another in love. Honor one another above yourselves." Romans 12:10 (NIV)

"…It (love) does not demand its own way. It is not irritable, and it keeps no record of being wronged." 1 Corinthians 13:5 (NLT)

Similar choices:

#14 Laugh at Yourself

#6 Have Fun Together

#37 Dream Big

31

31. Communicate Generously

In an article on FaithfulChoices.com, I pointed out the value of having fun as a family. Because we laugh together, we can share together. One of the comments a reader left encouraged me as a writer. It came from someone who's been married for 50 years.

She said,

"Love your blog and, you're right—we all have our different communication styles. My husband and I have just celebrated our 50th anniversary and we still love to look back to our family vacations at the Arizona dude ranch where every year we had some harrowing descents down those narrow mountain trails during our midnight rides.

Memorable, to say the least, and they forged some wonderful family memories! Love your blog and I'll be back!"

Sandra lit up my day when she wrote this.

Do you light up when people make a point of encouraging you by telling you positive things about yourself? I'll bet you do.

Our husbands or wives feel the same way. They want desperately to be included in the conversation, and not just to serve as a sounding board for our speech making moments.

Have you ever delivered the household speech? When someone does something in a way you consider unacceptable like eating without washing first, do you let loose a 20 minute sermon on the hidden dangers of not washing hands? I have.

Generous communication includes other voices. Occasionally, those other voices should speak more than our voice.

This excerpt from a letter written to a speaker in Calvin Miller's book, *The Empowered Communicator*[ix], meant to correct an errant public speaker, but it could easily apply to the overly vocal husband or wife.

Dear Speaker:

Your ego has become a wall between yourself and me. You're not really concerned about me, are you? You're mostly concerned about whether or not this speech is really working… You are so caught up in the issue of how I am going to receive your speech, you haven't thought of me much at all.

When I read it, I felt shattered.

I told myself when I made my household speech, that I spoke to help my family. As I ranted and raved, the reality became exposed. I did it for me.

John Maxwell shared in his book *Everyone Communicates, Few Connect*[x] three things people ask themselves whenever they hope to connect with someone. We become so comfortable with our loved ones; we forget the importance of the three questions. Whenever we communicate, let's seek to answer them for our spouse:

1. **Do you care for me?** You might think this is obvious, but for many couples it isn't. If it were, our rate of depression, divorce and drug abuse wouldn't be on the rise.

2. **Can you help me?** Sometimes help comes in the form of listening ears, which hold more value than the best deal on EBay. Being helpful involves more than a few words here and there, it means getting dirty, coming alongside and participating together.

3. **Can I trust you?** Repeated jokes at the expense of our children or spouse tear down the trust we long to build. Honoring one another matters. I remember when my kids were learning to swim. At some point, they each had to decide if

Momma could catch them. Have you caught someone you love lately? Husbands need trustworthy wives, wives need trustworthy husbands.

Generous communication starts by valuing the one we married.

To start, we must listen well, ask questions, share our similar values and build upon them. As a result, true connections get made.

God set the example for this kind of communication. In sending Jesus, He proved how much *He cares*. By giving an example in life and death, *He helps us*. He responds to our lives, gives us wisdom, and opens our eyes to His truth. Because of this, we know *we can trust Him*.

Jesus spoke of His desire to help us by using farming imagery. (They didn't have electrical outlets to show connection, they had grape vines.)

> "I am the vine; you are the branches. If you remain in me and I in you, you will bear much fruit; apart from me you can do nothing."
> John 15:5 (NIV)

If it mattered to God to generously communicate, it should matter to us.

Growth Questions:

- In what ways can you be more generous with your communication?

- Look at the questions above mentioned by John Maxwell. How do you seek those things when you listen to your spouse?

- In what ways has your husband or wife communicated generously with you?

Bible verses on this topic:

"Does not the ear test words as the tongue tastes food?" Job 12:11 (NIV)

"The soothing tongue is a tree of life, but a perverse tongue crushes the spirit." Proverbs 15:4 (NIV)

"But generous people plan to do what is generous, and they stand firm in their generosity." Isaiah 32:8 (NLT)

Similar choices:

#21 Be a Gift Giver

#27 Use Words

#48 Breeze It, Buzz It, Easy Does It

32

32. Keep Envy Out of Your Heart

Michael works all day at a corporate office where he's respected as the boss and people treat him with deference. He signs their paychecks and invests in them. When he comes home, he finds his wife Gina angry and tired. She's a stay-at-home mom with their three children: ages 3, 6, and 7.

He thinks, "She's been home all day, why does she get tired." He envies her free time. He resents how often she sees the children. This feeling stirs inside him whenever she makes a comment about working hard. He cannot see a connection between work and her home activities.

Gina appreciates his hard-earned financial support for the family, and yet, she can't help remembering when she was an accountant in an office. The employer and coworkers made her feel valued. It was straight forward. If she worked hard and finished according to plan, she received pay and occasionally bonuses.

She envies Michael's schedule; he gets paid, receives recognition, and has the ability to leave it all behind when returning home. As much as she loves her children, there is no leaving motherhood.

When he shares with her about office gossip or how he hopes to get a raise, she finds herself thinking, "When do I get a raise? At least you have other people to talk with, I'm on my own."

Ah, that little nasty beast of envy. Friendship with it acts like a root invading the pipes of our home, it blocks the flow of blessing God wants to give.

When it shoves anxious thoughts into our brains, we need to scoop them up and mentally dump them. We can tell it, "You aren't welcome here."

The choice challenges us daily. Many of us lack the strength to dump and clean those raging thoughts on our own. We can and should ask God to help us block or dump envious ideas that push their way into our hearts.

Being aware of our envy issues helps us keep the guard up. The following are common envies I've found:

House envy -- wanting what others have.

Car envy - wanting what others drive

Kid envy - wanting better behavior

Body envy - wanting someone else's body

Money envy - wanting a bigger paycheck

Toy envy - wanting the latest electronic or power gizmo

Marriage envy - wanting to have a marriage like someone else seems to have

With God's help, we can shoo envy out the door of our lives. His help is accessible in a moments notice. He's only a prayer away.

Growth Questions:

- Have you ever felt envy attempting to wrap its tentacles around your heart? What things cause you to feel envy?

- When do these feelings rise up the most often?

- Who do you envy?

- How can you involve God in this choice?

Bible verses on this topic:

"A heart at peace gives life to the body, but envy rots the bones."
Proverbs 14:30 (NIV)

"Then I observed that most people are motivated to success because they envy their neighbors. But this, too, is meaningless—like chasing the wind."
Ecclesiastes 4:4 (NLT)

"Let us not become conceited, provoking and envying each other."
Galatians 5:26 (NIV)

Similar choices:

#9 Bank on Marriage

#18 Beware of Joy Zappers

#29 Let Go of Self

33

33. Practice Patience

Something about living with and committing to the same person day and night, year after year, pushes us beyond our regular expectations. In marriage, we learn things about one another, some we like and don't like. Our patience gets tested.

Agnes accidentally created a hole in her shower wall one day. She told her husband Francis assuming he'd want to fix it. Nothing happened. Francis nodded and heard, but did nothing. Agnes felt frustrated and anxious. She didn't want to be annoying, but she was not thrilled with peaking into the back yard during a shower.

When we think about patience, our minds go to the times it gets tested. We think about when our husband or wife does that quirky little thing that we once thought was cute, but now find more irritating than we could have imagined. Living together and sharing our lives requires us to use patience.

What is patience?

Webster's online dictionary defines the word "patient" this way:

1: bearing pains or trials calmly or without complaint

2: manifesting forbearance under provocation or strain

3: not hasty or impetuous

4: steadfast despite opposition, difficulty, or adversity

5: able or willing to bear —used with of

Is this what God wants us to do?

As a wife, am I expected to simply bear the pains, not get impetuous, and remain steadfast? It doesn't sound fun; I thought marriage is supposed to be fun. Are you feeling a bit overwhelmed by this word, because I am?

Time to check out what the Hebrews (the language of the Old Testament) and Greeks (the language of the New Testament) thought about this word.

Using one of today's common translations, the New International Version, I only found "patient", "patiently," or "patience" three times in the Old Testament.

- "The end of a matter is better than its beginning, and patience is better than pride." Ecclesiastes 7:8 (NIV)
- "Be still before the Lord and wait patiently for him; do not fret when people succeed in their ways, when they carry out their wicked schemes." Psalm 37:7 (NIV)

- "I waited patiently for the Lord; he turned to me and heard my cry." Psalm 40:1 (NIV)

Based on the above verses alone, patience is the opposite of pride. It results in not feeling anxious. It expresses trust.

However, when I dug more, the words that are translated into "patient" or "patience" for English occur in other places. The same Hebrew or Greek word gets translated "forbear," "endure," and "wait."

This word indicates overcoming some sort of challenge, it also points toward the ability to stick to a goal, to keep going, no matter what. Could our lack of patience be found at the core of our divorce issues?

In the New Testament, we find verses where the word used gets defined as "hopeful endurance." It's translated as "suffering" and "steadfastness." We discover verses where it also means "perseverance."

Many people assume, "You'll know love when you find it." And yet, in 1 Corinthians 13:4 we find part of a detailed description of love.

The verse says, "Love is patient… "

In those three words, our ideas of marriage get challenged. Based on what we learn in the Bible about patience, we discover:

Love is the opposite of pride.

Love waits.

Love endures.

Love suffers long and doesn't complain.

Love is hopeful in endurance.

Love is steadfast.

Love perseveres.

I don't always want to do these things. I wish I could say I do, but I don't. I lose my patience more often than I like to admit. I don't always feel like suffering. I don't like to endure. Maybe you have the same difficulties.

Remember Agnes and Francis? Agnes decided to wait. As long as nothing entered the house through the hole and no mold formed, she would wait. It took a while. Keeping silent tested her ability to endure. A couple years later—yup, a couple of years—Francis asked if she wanted to help him fix the wall.

Due to finances, they tore out the wall themselves and replaced it. The whole shower now looks nicer and has been built stronger than it was before the hole. Their marriage is stronger too.

Let's remember, the Bible also says, "God is love." When the Bible tells us to be patient, it's also telling us God is patient. He does all these things for us. Because of it, He inspires us to want to be better. It's a lifelong adventure.

I will probably be working on this choice the rest of my life, but since I want my husband to treat me with patience, I believe it's time well spent.

Growth Questions:

- Which of the definitions of patience resonates most for you?

- Do you express this type of patience well? Why or why not?

- What steps or decisions can you make to work on building patience in your life?

Bible verses on this topic:

"Give thanks to the LORD, for he is good; his love endures forever."
1 Chronicles 16:34 (NIV)

"May the God who gives endurance and encouragement give you the same attitude of mind toward each other that Christ Jesus had," Romans 15:5 (NIV)

Similar choices:

#17 Set Aside Time for Togetherness

#7 Walk in Kindness

#28 Try, Try Again… In the Bedroom

34

34. Harness the Beast of Anger

My father brought me to rodeos as a child. I adored the thrill of watching a bronco rider getting flung around by choice. A cowboy straddled a wild horse. With one hand he grabbed onto the saddle, while attempting to keep his balance with the other and hugged the horse with his legs. The rider dreamt of remaining in the saddle longer than all the other riders. If he succeeded, he won.

In a bronco riding competition, there are two main riders in the arena. One rides a calm and controlled horse, and one gets tossed wildly on the bronco. It's an amazing irony to watch.

When horses are trained, or tamed, they all reject the first rider. Those who receive persistent and calm guidance eventually accept the harness, and a beautiful teamwork is created between horse and rider. A bronco, however, isn't tame. Therefore, teamwork is impossible.

One thing I've noticed about bronco riders, there aren't many old riders. Some learned from the beating and decided to stop, and some suffered tragic consequences. Let's not let that happen in our marriages.

Imagine our anger whirling and tossing within us, like a wild horse. We have a choice. We can be the rider who controls the anger or the one who gets tossed. In the interest of not having a hoof hit our loved ones, let's harness that sucker.

In order to become a person capable of calm, I believe we have to learn what causes our anger so that we learn how to tame it.

Books designed to help with this issue further include:

She's Gonna Blow (by Julie Ann Barnhill)

The Anger Workbook (by Les Carter and Dr. Frank Minirth)

Anger: Handling a Powerful Emotion in a Healthy Way (by Gary Chapman)

If you find yourself empathizing with the bronco, you'll need to learn what triggers your anger. This begins when you face it and discuss how it affects you. Depending upon how deep your anger goes, it may be worthwhile to consider counseling or coaching on this topic.

Counselors and coaches help us—when it comes to processing these untamed emotions—to discover where they come from so that we learn to control them rather than letting them control us.

If you are the spouse who gets kicked around verbally or physically, you too need someone to talk with. Just because you love broncos is no reason to get kicked in the ribs.

Growth Questions:

- What circumstances cause you to feel anger?

- How do you handle the anger when it comes?

- What steps could you take to begin harnessing that beast?

Bible verses on this topic:

"A gentle answer turns away wrath, but a harsh word stirs up anger." Proverbs 15:1 (NIV)

"For as churning cream produces butter, and as twisting the nose produces blood, so stirring up anger produces strife." Proverbs 30:33 (NIV)

"My dear brothers and sisters, take note of this: Everyone should be quick to listen, slow to speak and slow to become angry, because human anger does not produce the righteousness that God desires." James 1:19-20 (NIV)

Similar choices:

#10 Tame the Tongue

#44 Remove Rude From the 'Tude

#49 Learn the Secret

35

35. Devote Yourself to the Essentials

As a social media nut, I have helped churches and individuals build their communication skills online. I regularly search for organizations and individuals who create strong communication online. As I searched, I found an organization called Focus on the Family.

Focus on the Family is a Christian nonprofit organization which provides practical tools, spiritual resources and emotional support to families at every stage of life. It was started by family psychologist James Dobson in 1977. They have a strong voice many people trust and desire to hear on and offline.

While clicking through the various people I like on Facebook, I came across this comment from the Focus on the Family Facebook page:

"In your opinion, what's one essential for a good marriage?"

To this one, simple question, they received 2602 responses, 2584 "likes", and 259 shares. In the social media world, that's big.

By comparison, on the Walmart Facebook Page, when they posted a new picture for the Dog Days of Summer, they received 1472 "likes" and 99 comments.

Granted, this isn't scientific, but…

What did the comments say?

I went through every comment and discovered certain commonalities, the top three comments are here:

#1. God/Jesus

#2. Communication

#3. Trust

(Other contenders included: love, forgiveness, laughter, respect, prayer, friendship, honesty, and commitment.)

If these are the essentials to a life long marriage, would they be worth and investment of energy?

Growth Questions:

- Do you agree with the answers listed above?

- It's your turn... in your opinion, what's one essential for a good marriage?

- How do you demonstrate this thinking in your marriage?

Bible verses on this topic:

"But seek first his kingdom and his righteousness, and all these things will be given to you as well." Matthew 6:33 (NIV)

"May these words of my mouth and this meditation of my heart be pleasing in your sight, LORD, my Rock and my Redeemer." Psalm 19:14 (NIV)

Similar choices:

#52 Make God the Center of Your Marriage

#22 Sit on the Chair

#47 Hang onto the Rope of Hope

36

36. Spend Well

Money, money, money. We sweat for it. We dream of more. We believe in the options it seems to provide.

To us it means having the freedom to choose:

- a nicer home.
- a better car.
- a new cell phone.
- more nights at the movies.
- little league.
- fancy dinners, where we don't have to cook.

- dance classes
- designer clothes.
- free time.
- music and dancing.

When it gets waved around, it grabs our eyes like a flashlight on the floor to a dog.

How do I know?

My father grew up extremely poor. He believed money held the answer to all the woes of life. He worked nonstop: weekdays, weekends, whenever. He even rented gold dredging equipment and brought it with us on a family camping trip.

This same disease hits many people everyday. Like the insatiable belly of a sugar-addicted baby, we want it more and more and more.

Such passion, such drive. It's our treasure.

It becomes like a god to us.

According to a 2009 study at Utah State University [xi], couples who argue about money regularly run a higher risk of divorce in the future.

Want to test your faith in Christ? Decide to trust Him with your money more than you trust yourself.

Growth Questions:

- What does money mean to you?

- Is it tough to trust God with your money? Why?

- Have you and your spouse struggled with this issue? What can you do to change past patterns?

Bible verses on this topic:

"For where your treasure is, there your heart will be also."
Matthew 6:21 (NIV)

"Command those who are rich in this present world not to be arrogant nor to put their hope in wealth, which is so uncertain, but to put their hope in God, who richly provides us with everything for our enjoyment."
1 Timothy 6:17 (NIV)

Similar choices:

#11 The Dating Dilemma
#18 Beware of Joy Zappers
#49 Learn the Secret

"Listen to the mustn'ts, child.
Listen to the don'ts.
Listen to the shouldn'ts,
the impossibles, the won'ts.
Listen to the never haves,
then listen close to me...
Anything can happen, child.
Anything can be."
~ Shel Silverstein

FOURTH GEAR

Congratulations on travelling this far. You are clearly serious about moving forward in your marriage. Now, it's time to get out of your comfort zone and move into the big city. You've already been developing those strong basic habits which enable you to now move at high speeds. Not every corner announces itself as you pass. And yet, you still choose. If you miss one, you'll find yourself needing to turn around and try again.

37

37. Dream Big

If we allow our minds to wander, picturing the marriage of our dreams, what would it look like?

- Our every word is heard, valued, respected, received and responded to in such a way as to lighten our daily load.
- Romance, sex, and passion come to us exactly how we want it, when we want it, with genuine reciprocity.
- Having a partner whose heart and mind connects with ours, who roots for us no matter what.

(There's more, but you get the idea.)

Is this the stuff of dreams? Can it be real?

It depends on what you believe, and what you dream.

Marriage is messy. People aren't perfect. They yell, run, fight, close themselves off, and cry. They also comfort, encourage, excite, energize, appreciate and hope.

At my wedding, someone read these Bible verses:

"Two are better than one,

> because they have a good return for their labor:

If either of them falls down,

> one can help the other up.

But pity anyone who falls

> and has no one to help them up." Ecclesiastes 4:9-10 (NIV)

It doesn't sound very romantic, but neither is lying on the floor with no one to help you rise.

A friend of mine who has been happily married for forty years told me, "If you want a long marriage remember to give one hundred percent. If you both give 100%, the marriage will be strong. With a 50-50 arrangement you don't stand a chance." Having dealt with many serious life hardships—cancer, near death, children with health issues—he knew what he was saying.

My husband and I celebrated our 16th Anniversary this year. Is this the marriage of my dreams? I can honestly say, no.

I couldn't have dreamed the marriage I have. It's way better than my dreams. And it isn't thrust upon us like a gift. It involves effort and desire every single day.

Growth Questions:

- When was the last time you helped your spouse?

- Does your marriage fit your dreams?

- What can you do to make it stronger or appreciate what you have?

Bible verses on this topic:

"Trust in the Lord with all your heart; do not depend on your own understanding. Seek his will in all you do, and he will show you which path to take." Proverbs 3:5,6 (NIV)

"Give honor to marriage, and remain faithful to one another in marriage." Hebrews 13:4 (NIV)

Similar choices:

#3 Be Present

#17 Set Aside Time for Togetherness

7 Walk in Kindness

38

38. Be the Needle for Your Rose Bush

Anyone with rose bushes knows the power of those needles to deter someone who approaches. I grow roses in my yard, and I do not look forward to trimming them, because the needles form a fantastic defense.

With the people we love, we need to be their first line of defense. When someone puts them down, hurts them, or attacks their opinion whether we agree or disagree, we need to stand beside them.

We all want a supportive person in our lives; someone we trust to have our back when trouble comes. When we love our husband or wife, the proof of our love comes when we have the opportunity to protect them and stand up for their cause.

Many couples who remain together a long time let nothing negative escape their lips. For them, the marriage commitment means being best friends. They permit no outside force to bring down their marriage. They are the needle for their rose bush.

Growth Questions:

- Do you know people who share negative feelings about their spouse? How do you feel once this knowledge has been given to you?

- Have you ever felt tempted to tell someone about your husband or wife's annoying habits? What did you do?

- What strengths in your spouse can you focus on sharing with others?

A Bible verse on this topic:

"Do not let any unwholesome talk come out of your mouths, but only what is helpful for building others up according to their needs, that it may benefit those who listen." Ephesians 4:29 (NIV)

Similar choices:

#12 Don't Quit Yet

#50 Be the Good Wife

#51 Be the Good Husband

39

39. Face the Storms Together

When the storm clouds roll into town, the air is heavier, the mood changes, and people respond according to their expectations.

For Alyssa and Aaron, their storm took the form of a niece who passed away suddenly. For Frank and Belle, their storm's name was Cancer, breast cancer to be specific. For Lil and Matthew, their storm meant losing their home.

Storms bring out our worst and our best.

Some of us hide out and hope for the sun to return. Others attempt to ignore the change, and live as if nothing were different. A third group embraces rain; they look for the good and usually find it.

For the first crowd, rain brings fatigue, sadness and a sense of doom and gloom. Alyssa and Aaron hid out from the world. They stopped calling friends, they stopped attending church. They shut down from other people and from each other.

In marriage, when the storms roll in, some of us see only the negative. The eyes of this group remain on the rain or hail or lightening spewing out of the trials they face. This crowd sees only trouble.

The second group—like Southern Californians during the first rain—convinces themselves nothing is wrong. They drive as if the sun still shines, and many of them crash.

When Belle learned of the cancer within her body, she didn't want to think about it or talk about it. She just kept doing all the same things she had been doing. Frank figured it must not be so bad if Belle didn't acknowledge the problem. He stopped asking about it. He went away with the guys and left her alone to cry at the thought of chemotherapy. By the time he returned, she didn't want to talk with him or even see him.

When a marital storm comes, it's still a storm and should be respected as such. It requires patience and persistence.

The last group adores a good storm for multiple reasons. Lil and Matthew certainly didn't like losing their home, but they figured they needed to learn how to handle money better. They asked for help from friends who gave them a place to live for a while. They sought direction from their church leaders. The pastor advised them to learn some money management skills through a program available locally.

Over time, they saved and learned. They did move out on their own again, with closer friends and wiser hearts and minds.

Whether it's the change in temperature, the precious water given to the plants, animals and people, or a great opportunity to go puddle hopping, some people welcome storms. In marriage, the question isn't IF we'll face storms, but WHEN we'll face them. We need Christ as our umbrella. To protect us and make us wise.

The rain will come, because it must. Without it, we'd all live in the barren desert. Marital storm lovers recognize this season as a time of growth and potential prosperity for those who are wise.

When our marriages encounter storms, if we hunt for the possible, the pluses of the moment, we'll find them. In the end, we'll receive what happens after every storm… growth. Our marriages will become stronger because of our willingness to accept, endure, walk wisely and seek puddles.

Growth Questions:

- Think of storms you've faced in your life, either in marriage or prior to marriage. Which group fits your style of storm dweller?

- Do you want to change this style or are you content with it? Why?

- Are you facing any storms today? What can you do in the midst of your storm to seek the pluses of the moment?

Bible verses on this topic:

"Consider it pure joy, my brothers and sisters, whenever you face trials of many kinds," James 1:2 (NIV)

"We can rejoice, too, when we run into problems and trials, for we know that they help us develop endurance. And endurance develops strength of character, and character strengthens our confident hope of salvation. And this hope will not lead to disappointment. For we know how dearly God loves us, because he has given us the Holy Spirit to fill our hearts with his love." Romans 5:3-5 (NLT)

Similar choices:

#26 Face Your Fears

#12 Don't Quit Yet

#18 Beware of Joy Zappers

40

40. Refuse to Make Pride Your Buddy

When my father took me snow skiing as a child, he began teaching me to not fear falling. For skiers, falling happens as much as, or more than the skiing itself. They embrace it. At the end of the day, they get together to share their most incredible wipe outs.

The skill of falling helps skiers in a fundamental way. Those who fight the fall, because they're too proud or think they're too strong, end up getting hurt. When they let go of their pride and relax into it, they get to ski the next day, unless they were moving at breakneck speeds or flying through the air.

People who ski for years have discovered and appreciated how to relax into a fall. But, when someone gets too full of themselves or too terrified, they fear the fall.

An old expression says, "Pride goes before a fall." I think that's because once your body is strewn across the floor, a big head gets deflated.

When describing the nature of love, the Bible states, "it is not proud," in 1 Corinthians 13:4. This confuses us, because we often consider pride to be a good thing, a way of supporting those we love. We say things like, "Honey, I'm proud of you," as encouragement and support.

But when the Apostle Paul wanted the people of Corinth to see the problem of pride, he spoke about arrogance. The Greek word he used, fusioo, meant, "to inflate, to blow up, or to cause to swell up."

In other words, Paul was saying that love isn't fat headed.

Let's be real with our loved ones by falling in front of them. If we always try to place ourselves in the best light, we're fooling ourselves. Even the prettiest princess gets the sniffles.

I took my first marital dive on our honeymoon. We stayed in a cute bed and breakfast in Northern California. A couple days into it, my allergies attacked fiercely. My eyes watered, snot oozed out my nose, and I had to carry tissues everywhere.

Talk about taking a fall. At the wedding, I wore a gorgeous dress and had my hair and makeup applied by professionals. I felt as if I were real life princess. Then, only a few days later I resembled a relative of Jabba the Hut. I might have even sounded like him.

One particular morning I woke to discover both my eyes had swollen to the size of golf balls. I started crying with whatever tears could make their way through my flesh. "Why did you marry me? I look hideous," I said while staring at myself in the mirror.

It was one of those moments when Tim got to prove himself, and he did. He declared his love regardless of the moment. He proved it by holding my hand and helping me see my way through the front door. The swelling decreased, but my trust in Tim increased.

When we become so busy building up own sense of pride, the world centers on us. How can we really love others if we're so in love with ourselves? Our spouses need to know the love continues beyond beauty, brains, successes or failures.

As we let go of this type of pride, we also let go of our own need for temporary achievement. We'll learn to ask one another for help, we lift one another, and work together rather than apart.

This puffed up pride makes the foundation of the marriage weak. If we want strong friendships with our husbands or wives, it's not worth the pain of trying to balance a giant brain. When we learn not to fear the fall, we invite our spouses to help us and encourage us.

Great skiers wipe out, they also help one another.

Growth Questions:

- Have you admitted your own strengths and weaknesses? If so, what are they?

- What strengths or weaknesses do you appreciate in your spouse?

- How can you learn to relax when you fall? (Not if, because we all fall.)

Bible verses on this topic:

"In his pride the wicked man does not seek him; in all his thoughts there is no room for God." Psalm 10:4 (NIV)

"A fool's mouth lashes out with pride, but the lips of the wise protect them." Proverbs 14:3 (NIV)

"For everything in the world—the lust of the flesh, the lust of the eyes, and the pride of life—comes not from the Father but from the world." 1 John 2:16 (NIV)

Similar choices:

#12 Don't Quit Yet

#38 Be the Needle for Your Rose Bush

#29 Let Go of Self

41

41. Listen Up

Diane stored the events of her day inside her head. When Stephen came home, she began pouring it out. She shared how the kids spilled soda all over the floor, how her mother wanted them to come to visit next month, and what her work friends talked about at lunch. She shared her favorite bits of the daily news and why her feet hurt badly.

About an hour later, Diane and Stephen sat on their couch together. The kids had gone to bed. Diane mentioned the soda incident. Stephen's eyes glazed over, not knowing what she is talking about. This is where the conversation went very bad.

It makes us want to scream when the one we love most doesn't listen.

How can we change this scenario?

1) Simplify the thinking.

Twitter succeeds because people like short and sweet information bits. We have so much noise around us every day. It's not because we don't care, and it's not because we aren't interested. We simply cannot hear the details of a full day in the time span of a half hour and be expected to recall everything.

I'm not innocent on this one.

My husband likes to say "Phew!" after I unload a whole day onto his tired lap. He sits on the couch to breathe his first calm breath in many hours, and I dump my day onto him. Information overload.

2) Lather, Rinse, Repeat.

Ever read the side of a shampoo bottle? The directions read: lather, rinse, repeat.

Repeat? How often? Every time we re-enter the shower. Hair gets dirty; it needs shampoo… so we repeat. The same is true in communication.

We talk, listen, connect and repeat, over and over as long as we both shall live. We need to repeat ourselves.

Sometimes, we place an imagined value on our words, like they're pieces of gold. They're so precious. Why would anyone, especially the beloved people in our lives, drop even one?

Let's flip that little thought upside down. If our words are like gold, so are theirs. How often have we dropped one? Important topics require repetition. Embrace it for the communication bridge it is.

When we repeat, let's be cautious. It's tempting to build an angry or sarcastic attitude. I don't know about you, but for me, when sarcasm is used, I tend to close my ears.

3) Throw in some sugar with that spice.

When we say complimentary things or verbally notice successes, it's like conversational sugar.

Unfortunately, the people we love often hear our harshest comments, our spice. Maybe, it's because we believe they'll be around long after others go, but too many spicy words can pickle the strongest of relationships.

How we treat the people we love affects their ability or desire to listen when we talk. If you think about it, the same is true for us. We shut down and stop listening to people who regularly deliver spice to our ears.

The kinder we treat others with our words; the more likely they are to recall what we say. It's worth adding the sugar.

Growth Questions:

- When you talk with your spouse, do you ever cluster things together like Diane?

- Which of the ideas expressed above connected with you the most?

- What can you do today to improve your communication style?

Bible verses on this topic:

"May these words of my mouth and this meditation of my heart be pleasing in your sight, LORD, my Rock and my Redeemer." Psalm 19:14 (NIV)

"To answer before listening—that is folly and shame." Proverbs 18:13 (NIV)

"Do to others whatever you would like them to do to you. This is the essence of all that is taught in the law and the prophets." Matthew 7:12 (NLT)

Similar choices:

#10 Tame the Tongue

#41 Listen Up

#46 Back Off Boasting Words

42

42. Don't Dance for the Devil

In Greek mythology, a woman named Pandora was given a box she should not open. When she gave into temptation and opened it, she released all forms of evil into the world.

In our marriage, when we say things like, "I told you so" or "I knew it", we are celebrating something bad that has occurred. In essence, we let loose all forms of evil to dance around our home. At first it seems funny or interesting to see, but it damages the love we long to find.

Some couples secretly rejoice when the partner fails. Maybe it's because they brag or taunt one another. For Ezra, it's because Mary never celebrated his success. When he got a raise at work, she nodded. Then, she made comments about how little it really was.

He heard these comments; saw the rolling eyes, the raised eyebrows. When a coworker took her idea and claimed it as their own, he found himself saying things like, "Are you sure it was your idea? Really?"

When something goes wrong for someone we love, if we celebrate the problem, we help cause a new problem. Our grandmas used to say, "If we can't say anything good, don't say anything at all."

My grandparents were happily married for over fifty years. Their advice is worth following.

Growth Questions:

- Have you ever found yourself rejoicing when someone else failed?

- Why did you feel happy for their sadness?

- Has your spouse ever felt this same attitude?

- How can you choose to think or speak differently?

Bible verses on this topic:

"Love does not delight in evil but rejoices in the truth"
1 Corinthians 13:6 (NIV)

"A gossip betrays a confidence, but a trustworthy person keeps a secret."
Proverbs 11:13 (NIV)

Similar choices:

#10 Tame the Tongue

#34 Harness the Beast of Anger

#44 Remove Rude from the 'Tude

43

43. Count the Pluses

When we find ourselves falling in love, the reasons we fall don't matter. Or do they?

Remember that rushing, gushing feeling of the heart throbbing against the chest, the fingers tingling for the chance to touch our beloved one, our mad love affair with love begins; adrenaline and dopamine flood the brain. It's a rush, like leaping off a cliff into a cool pool of water. It's exhilarating.

We want to spend every moment together, until... the effects wear off.

For some of us it takes longer, but one day we find ourselves married to a regular person who does regular person stuff, complete with annoying habits we never thought we would link to our lives. Now, we face a decision.

We've reached a corner.

When Tim married me, he knew I lacked basic cleanliness and cooking skills. That's right, he married a slob who could barely cook. What was he thinking?

He could have regularly pointed out these problems. He would have been correct. Yet, he didn't. Never once has he complained about a meal I made. As a result, I evaluated them for myself. I wanted to get better so that I liked my own cooking. He also never complained about things strewn across the floor.

You know what Tim did? He bragged about me. Told the people at work about things I wrote or places I spoke. He shared the stuff he loved, not the stuff that bugged him. Because of it, I wanted to become more like the things he loved.

When we discover the faults of our spouse, we can glare at them over and over, re-examine them and turn them inside out. We can point to them time and time again. Reminding the other person how short they fall from our initial idea of their perfection.

Or.

We can brag to others and notice the pluses. The more we tell them how they please us, the more we believe it.

Growth Questions:

- How do you talk to your husband or wife?

- How do you talk about your husband or wife?

- What kind words could you begin to use today?

Bible verses on this topic:

"Be joyful. Grow to maturity. Encourage each other. Live in harmony and peace. Then the God of love and peace will be with you."
2 Corinthians 13:11 (NLV)

"Don't use foul or abusive language. Let everything you say be good and helpful, so that your words will be an encouragement to those who hear them." Ephesians 4:29 (NLV)

Similar choices:

#19 Support One Another, Especially in Tough Times

#9 Bank on Marriage

#47 Hang on to the Rope of Hope

44

44. Remove Rude from the 'Tude

Marta considers sarcasm her love language. By that, she means, whenever her husband Matthias makes a kind comment, she gives him a clever retort. At first Matthias thought it showed her intelligence. Then, he found it cute and clever. But over time it felt hurtful and mean.

At some point, we acquired the idea that mouthing off at those we love makes us cool or funny. When we react sarcastically to everyday statements to make ourselves seem smarter or wittier, we actually whack away at the self-esteem of our loved ones.

We cut into them with our remarks, because we think it's clever. They laugh to seem unscathed, but damage has been done. At some point, after multiple rude comments, our spouse will throw their own spear at us.

It always hurts to be on the receiving end of a sarcastic spear. Knowing the feeling should inspire us to pull our arm back and find another way to communicate. Those we love deserve better.

Growth Questions:

- Do you have any favorite sarcastic responses? What are they?

- Why do you like these comments?

- Do you know what it feels like to be on the receiving end of a rude comment? What did you think from this perspective?

Bible verses on this topic:

"Answering before listening is both stupid and rude."
Proverbs 18:13 (The Message)

"Some people make cutting remarks, but the words of the wise bring healing."
Proverbs 12:18 (NIV)

"If you're dumb enough to call attention to yourself by offending people and making rude gestures, Don't be surprised if someone bloodies your nose. Churned milk turns into butter; riled emotions turn into fist fights."
Proverbs 30:32-33 (The Message)

Similar choices:

#10 Tame the Tongue

#45 Forgive Often

#42 Don't Dance for the Devil

45

45. Forgive often

"But I'm right, I know I'm right, and that's how it is!"

Ever feel like saying this?

Did it help?

The value of forgiveness looms large within the Bible. The things being forgiven from cover to cover encompass pretty yucky stuff.

-Joseph's brothers begged for forgiveness for selling him into slavery.

-David asked for forgiveness when he killed a guy to get the girl.

-Peter sought forgiveness when he denied knowing Jesus.

-Jesus forgave the people who murdered Him.

-God forgives us when we repeatedly mess up and sin against Him daily.

-The Apostle Peter quizzed Jesus to know how often we should be willing to forgive. He asked Jesus, "Lord, how many times shall I forgive my brother or sister who sins against me? Up to seven times?" Matthew 18:21 (NIV)

Jesus answered,

"I tell you, not seven times, but seventy-seven times." Matthew 18:22 (NIV)

In marriage, we discover pretty ugly parts in each other, because all of us contain ugly parts. We see habits in our spouse we don't enjoy, hear expressions that bother us, and witness another human being sinning before God.

One of the biggest troubles within marriage is lack of forgiveness.

In the Bible, we rarely see the idea of "what goes around comes around" but we do when it comes to forgiveness.

Jesus said,

"Do not judge, and you will not be judged. Do not condemn, and you will not be condemned. Forgive, and you will be forgiven." Luke 6:37 (NIV)

God gives clear direction on this.

"Bear with each other and forgive one another if any of you has a grievance against someone. Forgive as the Lord forgave you." Colossians 3:13 (NIV)

What happens when we forgive?

The boulder on our back moves, the pressure lessens, we learn to enjoy each other again. Stanford University Medical Center did research in 1999 on the topic of forgiveness. They determined the value of learning forgiveness in coping with life stresses. It improves our outlook in all parts of life.

It's not a quick fix, it takes time, but so does real forgiveness. Our marriages deserve this attention. It is possible to forgive someone for even the worst of offenses, but not because we are such wonderful people. This kind of forgiveness only comes from God. With the strength He gives, we can do it.

Growth Questions:

- Have you ever been forgiven? How did it feel?

- Are you harboring resentment against your spouse? If so, why?

- Have you asked God to help you to become more forgiving? If not, do so now.

A Bible verse on this topic:

"Bear with each other and forgive one another if any of you has a grievance against someone. Forgive as the Lord forgave you." Colossians 3:13 (NIV)

Similar choices:

#19 Support One Another, Especially When It's Tough

#31 Communicate Generously

#29 Let Go of Self

46

46. Back Off the Boasting Words

Years ago I watched a TV show about a strong minded and verbally aggressive reporter named *Murphy Brown*. In one episode, a few friends from the news room spoke about how they met her. They mentioned her beauty and the way she confidently walked into a room. As they shared, they each said, "And then she spoke."

The mouth. It's a powerful tool.

It produces beautiful expressions like "honey," "handsome," "sweetheart" and "lover." It also packs the punch of Mike Tyson in his hay day, given half a chance.

We don't have to attack those we love to cause major damage; we can claim to know things they don't. We can stomp our loved ones to pieces with a pious know-it-all and done-it-all approach.

When a woman refers to her husband as a spare child, it's boasting about her own superiority as an "adult." (Sorry ladies, it's true.) When men taunt women with their strength, their paycheck, or their technical abilities, that's boasting.

Verbal signs of boasting include expressions like:

- "I told you so."
- "What were you thinking?"
- "That's right, I said it."
- "Talk to the hand." (Does anyone still say that?)

Well, you get the idea.

Out of the genuine love we feel and act upon, we can clamp our lips shut and block those boasts before they begin.

Growth Questions:

- What boasts are most likely to escape your lips?

- Why would you want to boast to the most important person in your life?

- How can you seek to clamp your lips when those boasts long to burst forth?

Bible verses on this topic:

"This is what the LORD says: "Let not the wise boast of their wisdom or the strong boast of their strength or the rich boast of their riches,"
Jeremiah 9:23 (NIV)

"Do not boast about tomorrow, for you do not know what a day may bring."
Proverbs 27:1 (NIV)

"Instead, God chose things the world considers foolish in order to shame those who think they are wise. And he chose things that are powerless to used them to bring to nothing what the world considers important. As a result, no one can ever boast in the presence of God." 1 Corinthians 1:27-29 (NLT)

Similar choices:

#27 Use Words

#31 Communicate Generously

#20 Give a Shout Out

47

47. Hang Onto the Rope of Hope

The first time I went rock climbing, I knew nothing about it. A guide told me how to hook up my rope. He climbed ahead of me. A friend held the rope below, while the guide directed from above.

I began to climb with every intention of success. Half-way up the rock face, my eyesight and muscles combined to convince me I could go no further. My guide yelled down for me to hold the rope; he'd lift me the necessary two inches to reach another hand hold.

I believed he could do it. I held onto the rope of hope as he yanked my body up. I felt myself pulled the necessary distance to reach the next hand hold. An inch isn't much, but it was everything to me as I hung in pain on the side of Camelback Mountain.

In our marriages, there always comes a time when we believe in our husband or wife or not. To prove our belief, we literally grab the rope of hope and let them do the lifting. In the end, they get stronger and our trust increases, if we willingly take the risk.

Heads up though, the time will come when they'll be clinging to that same rope and you will be the lifter.

If we choose to make Christ the center of our marriage, when it seems like neither of us have the strength to do the heavy lifting, He comes alongside us and enables us to achieve more than we can imagine. If we ask, He provides the rope of hope to help us reach a spot where we can continue to climb.

Another thing I learned from this climbing day—the wise climber always secures the rope, whether they think they'll need it or not. In the same way, Jesus is our ever present help in times of need.

Growth Questions:

- In your marriage, have you ever trusted your wife to lift you at a time when you felt too tired to continue? How did it work?

- Have you ever lifted your husband when they felt tired by life?

- How can you both trust God even if you find it difficult to trust one another?

Bible verses on this topic:

"But if we hope for what we do not yet have, we wait for it patiently." Romans 8:25 (NIV)

"Guide me in your truth and teach me, for you are God my Savior, and my hope is in you all day long." Psalm 25:5 (NIV)

"'For I know the plans I have for you,' says the LORD. 'They are plans for good and not for disaster, to give you a future and a hope." Jeremiah 29:11 (NLT)

Similar choices:

#52 Make God the Center of Your Marriage

#4 Believe in Change

#22 Sit on the Chair

48

48. Breeze It, Buzz It, Easy Does It

In the musical *West Side Story*, my favorite song came before the big fight at the end. If you've seen the show, you know the one I mean. A crowd of teenage boys, packed up with so much angst, anger and hormonal energy that it practically oozes out their pores, prepare to fight one another.

They don't want to lose their tempers. So, they keep telling themselves, "Keep cool boy, real cool."

If you know the show, this doesn't work. They don't keep cool.

Many of us have the same problem. We don't keep cool. When someone says something against our beliefs or our point of view, we lower the hammer on their heads.

It doesn't work any better for us than it did for the boys in *West Side Story*.

Jesus had people coming after him and taunting him very early in His ministry. Over and over people tried to push his anger button. They wanted Him to let loose on someone.

Jesus kept His cool under extreme circumstances. He got whipped and kept His cool. He was spit on and kept His cool. He suffered on the cross AND kept His cool.

He knew the temptation to scream and bellow. In one Bible story, we get a glimpse of the potential of His temper.

Jesus was hungry and passed by a fig tree. When He noticed no fruit growing on it, He said, *"May you never bear fruit again!"* The tree immediately withered and died. You can read the story in Matthew 21:18-20.

We often read this as a side note, an unimportant story. I think it shows what would happen if He released His anger on those who persecuted Him. Devastation.

Jesus was completely capable of causing destruction. And yet, *He preferred a softer, gentler approach.*

He turned the other cheek. He answered without yelling. He listened. He kept His cool.

Imagine what could happen if you chose to do the same. In your marriage, following a long day, your tired spouse foolishly says something harsh. What if you calmly responded? What if you talk with her gently even though there is a stirring of anger inside you?

Like the boys in *West Side Story*, one tense movement excites another tense movement. Before you know it, there are dead bodies strewn about the neighborhood. Okay, that's a bit extreme, but many of us do kill our relationships by pummeling those we love with our verbal capabilities.

Genuine coolness is not something you can do on our own. Especially if a part of you likes that adrenaline rush of anger. With God's help, you can train yourselves to give the gentle answer instead of the attacking one. He knows the temptation. He's been there. He can help.

Growth Questions:

- Do you know anyone who reacts harshly when the pressures of life come?

- Have you been guilty of giving a harsh word? What did you do?

- What can you do right now to find a better sense of cool?

Bible verses on this topic:

"A gentle answer turns away wrath, but a harsh word stirs up anger." Proverbs 15:1 (NIV)

"Which do you choose? Should I come with a rod to punish you, or should I come with love and a gentle spirit?" 1 Corinthians 4:21 (NLT)

"Be completely humble and gentle; be patient, bearing with one another in love." Ephesians 4:2 (NIV)

Similar choices:

#10 Tame the Tongue

#34 Harness the Beast of Anger

#42 Don't Dance for the Devil

"Do you wish to rise?
Begin by descending.
You plan a tower that will pierce the clouds?
Lay first the foundation of humility."
~Saint Augustine

Fifth Gear

You've hit the marital highway. At this speed, the corners take planned effort or you'll drive miles out of your way. These are the foundational chorners that will help your marriage survive. If you don't know and utilize them, you'll be headed for a high speed accident with multiple injuries. But, if you choose wisely, these choices are the ones that pack the biggest power. No risk, no reward.

49

49. Learn the Secret

Mike has been employed by the same company since he started working at the age of 18. He became a stock boy at a grocery store. Over time, he eventually worked his way toward cashier and over time became the store's manager. He's been at the store for 20 years. He has no reason to complain, and yet he finds himself thinking, "Is this as good as it gets?"

Marissa married her husband in her twenties. She knew she wanted to marry him. They both like athletics. They both enjoy movies. They can talk for hours. They married, and their life became the American dream: two kids, two dogs, and two cars.

She spends most of her time cleaning house, cooking, and helping their children. She still loves her husband and adores her kids, but her mind wanders. She often finds herself thinking, "Is this as good as it gets?"

Maybe roles are switched for you. Maybe you both work, or you are both out of work. However it breaks down for you, the question still comes up. Is this as good as it gets?

We ask this question because we expected something more dramatic, something more exciting. Regular life is regular, even boring. We wonder why we can't have the life of the characters on our latest favorite TV show. Why don't we own and drive that fancy car we passed in the car lot?

We tell ourselves that if we got the new job, or new house, or new car, or nicer clothes life would be better, more exciting. Some of us do get the car and discover it's a car. It still gets flat tires. It still runs out of gas. It's a car, and life isn't better.

The same happens with all the other stuff too. The house is a house, and it always needs work. The clothes are clothes, which have to get replenished regularly. While we may feel elated for a moment, this feeling passes. Our lives become regular and boring.

Some of you are talking to me now. You're saying things like, "I wish I had the chance to see for myself." or "That's easy for you to say, Paula."

All the smiling faces in the advertising can't be lying. We picture them in our heads. We assume it will one day happen to us. We'll burst with joy at some new purchase.

What if someone had it all? What if that person got respect and authority? He lived a wealthy, empowered life.

Then, the tables turned. The same person lost it all: the home, the car, everything. If he found contentment after having lost everything, would his point of view be worth hearing?

This did happen. The man's name was Paul. He came from a Roman family. We don't know the details, but we know he received respect and authority. He was trusted to do extreme things at a young age. Then, his life changed. He walked away from the respect and power. He became homeless, a wanderer, a jailbird. It all happened because He wanted to please God instead of himself.

This same man said,"I know what it is to be in need, and I know what it is to have plenty. I have learned the secret of being content in any and every situation, whether well fed or hungry, whether living in plenty or in want. I can do all this through him who gives me strength." Philippians 4:12,13 (NIV)

Want to know what he was doing when he made this statement? He was in jail.

Paul declared his contentment while under guard. Does this sound odd to you? It does to me. Earlier in this book of the Bible, which was a letter to the people who followed Jesus in the town of Philippi, he shared what happened.

"Now I want you to know, brothers and sisters, that what has happened to me has actually served to advance the gospel. As a result, it has become clear throughout the whole palace guard and to everyone else that I am in chains for Christ. And because of my chains, most of the brothers and sisters have become confident in the Lord and dare all the more to proclaim the gospel without fear." Philippians 1:12-14 (NIV)

To Paul's way of thinking, he was serving others while he was imprisoned. This was his secret of contentment. He loved to serve God and others. He told us to do it too.

No matter what our life circumstance, well-fed or in need, our willingness to serve others brings about a change. The change happens from within and our eyes open to the goodness of God where we are, in our regular everyday world.

It gets better, in life and in marriage, when we choose to serve others. It certainly did for Paul.

Growth Questions:

- Have you found yourself thinking like Mike or Marrissa? Is this as good as it gets?

- How can you serve your spouse today?

- What's holding you back?

Bible verses on this topic:

"You, my brothers and sisters, were called to be free. But do not use your freedom to indulge the flesh; rather, serve one another humbly in love." Galatians 5:13 (NIV)

"I can do all this through him who gives me strength." Philippians 4:13 (NIV)

Similar choices:

#19 Support One Another, Especially When It's Tough

#15 Serving is Loving

#33 Practice Patience

50

50. Be The Good Wife

I have no illusions of my own wifely grandeur. "Perfection is not mine," declares Paula. So, how can I possibly address the topic of a "good wife"? Good question. So glad you asked.

I decided to ask some of my male friends with wonderful marriages to see what they said about their good wives.

- "[She is]beautiful, calm and unflappable. When I got sick I learned how loyal and caring she really is. I don't know what I would do without her."

- "Sweet personality, has a good sense of humor, great mom, fun to be with, loving, tender soul, believer…"

- "Loyal, trustworthy, her unconditional love for the kids and I. Truly a blessing in my life in so many ways. She taught me about God and that just being a good person is not good enough."
- "In spite of the difficult times we've gone through, she has always been supportive and calm."

I didn't ask my own husband, because it would be too self-serving, but found the words these men shared interesting.

Men have been hunting for good wives since the beginning of time.

Adam had it easy, but from that point on it's been tough. The Bible contains a memorable chapter about a woman of noble character (aka a good wife). King Lemuel's mother taught him what to look for in a woman. She gave him intense details.

I thought about including the whole chapter here for you to read and then explain it, but it's pretty long and not everyone wants to read every detail. If you are a detail person, it's found in Proverbs 31.

Now, in the words of the amazing Inigo Montoya (from *The Princess Bride*), "Let me 'splain… no, there is too much, let me sum up."

The king's mother wanted the best for her son. Here's what she told him to look for put in present terms:

A Woman of Noble Character (aka the Good Wife) is:

- Kind

- Good at shopping and finding deals. (That's right, God meant us to be good shoppers.)
- A hard worker.
- A capable business woman.
- Generous.
- A capable care-giver to her family.
- A good money manager.
- A multi-tasker.
- Helpful to other people.
- Strong and dignified.
- Able to laugh at herself and life.
- Wise.
- Guided by her faith.
- Aware of God's power compared to her capability.
- Worth mentioning.

Hand to head, dramatic pause. Can we all say, "Oy vay?" What a list this is!

I feel as if I can claim a few for myself, but certainly not all and not all the time. What about you?

It's important to remember, this is a mother's advice to her son on who to look for when deciding to get married. If you have a son, wouldn't you want him to go hunting for this type of lady? I would.

I wonder if she would claim all these traits about herself too.

To be fair, nothing on this list is wrong or evil in anyway. A woman who could and would do it all deserves the comments made about her at the end of this chapter in Proverbs.

> "Honor her for all that her hands have done, and let her works bring her praise at the city gate." Proverbs 31:31 (NIV)

It's easy to see this list and feel as if its unachievable, not worth the effort. I prefer to use it as a guideline. It helps me to see areas of strength and places where I can improve.

We can all learn from the details found here.

Growth Questions:

- (For the men) What makes your wife a good wife?

- (For the ladies) Which of the listed items do you do best? What needs work?

Bible verses on this topic:

"A wife of noble character who can find? She is worth far more than rubies. Her husband has full confidence in her and lacks nothing of value."

Proverbs 31: 10-11 (NIV)

Similar choices:

#4 Believe in Change

#20 Give a Shout Out

#51 The Good Husband

51

51. Be the Good Husband

I adore hearing women brag about their husbands. It lightens my heart to know how many brag-worthy men exist. I've also heard many who attack their husbands or belittle them.

Have you heard these comments?

When we get into us versus them, neither one wins. Once we've bonded together into our girl power cluster, guys don't stand a chance. It's too bad. We end up hurting ourselves in the process.

Certainly some men don't deserve praise for their behavior, but I've noticed the more we focus on negative the more we see negative. It happens at work. The employee who only receives discouraging comments tends to become more discouraged. It happens with our children. The child who repeatedly hears their failings tends to embrace failure more than success.

With this thought in mind, let's choose to brag on him.

Since I have only one "him", here we go.

What makes Tim a good husband?

- He seeks me out every day and makes sure we pray together.
- He cleans the cat litter.
- He never complains about my food, even though it sometimes deserves it.
- He kisses me every day when we part one another's company and when we come together again.
- He calls me "gorgeous" every day.
- He reads to our children each night.
- He supports me when I tell our kids stuff. (We talk later if he disagrees.)
- He helps wash the dishes and encourages the kids to do it too.
- He wants to read books together (sometimes).
- He understands my lack of desire to watch Formula One racing.
- He occasionally sits through Food TV shows with me.
- He's my best friend.
- He loves God and trusts Him as much or more than I do.

(There's more, but you get the idea.)

It's tempting to feel nauseated when someone starts getting all goody-goody like this, but God desires for us to be positive about the people in our lives. It enhances the strength of our relationship.

Men, check out that list. Do you feel as if you have many brag worthy attitudes and actions. Give your lady a little help here. Be the man who is worth bragging about. When you desire to be the kind of man God wants you to be, when you make the effort to please Him, you make it easy for her to brag on you.

If you want to be a brag-worthy husband, start with one action at a time. Researchers have discovered that our actions often precede our thinking. So, take a clue from the list above or consult your lady on what she'd like to brag about. Then, begin to become that person one action at a time. Before you know it, you'll be glancing back at the past realizing how much you've grown. And, you might even like it.

Growth Questions:

- (For the women) What makes your husband a good husband?

- (For the men) What can you do to become the good husband?

Bible verses on this topic:

"Therefore encourage one another and build each other up, just as in fact you are doing." 1 Thessalonians 5:11 (NIV)

"Husbands, love your wives, just as Christ loved the church and gave himself up for her." Ephesians 5:25 (NIV)

Similar choices:

#27 Use Words

37 Dream Big

#50 Be the Good Wife

52

52. Make God the Center of Your Marriage

It seems obvious to say in a Christian book about marriage, but many marriages miss this point. I cannot over state the value of making God the center of your marriage. Over and over, when I talk with couples who live through traumatic experiences and not only remain together but grow stronger, they tell me, "God did it, not us."

When Tim proposed to me, he started us on a path I couldn't have expected. As we stood peering over the side of the Queen Mary in Long Beach, California, he said, "Are you okay with being number 2 in my life?"

Of course, you can imagine the stunned look on my face. Why would anyone want to be number 2 in a relationship? I had to ask him what he meant. In response he said, "If God is number one, are you okay with being number 2."

Being number 2 to the Creator of the Universe doesn't sound like a horrible spot to me. Plus, I valued God's opinion over Tim's too. As you can guess, I agreed. But, I didn't have a clue what that would mean each day in our marriage. .

According to leading researchers, faith does make a difference, but only within specific boundaries.

The National Marriage Project organized by the University of Virginia releases a publication each year entitled *"The State of Our Unions, Marriage in America."* [xii] (It's free and worth a read.)

This self-described, "nonprofit, nonpartisan organization dedicated to strengthening families and civil society in the U.S. and the world," stated one area of their studies as "the most powerful religious predictor of marital success."

By asking pointed questions, they discovered one thing that helps marriages stick together like super glue on steroids.

I'm sure you've guessed what it is. They wrote that couples who state, "God is the center of our marriage," are 26% more likely to claim to be "Very Happy" in marriage than all other Christians (that's 76% -husbands, and 77% – wives), with only 1% of husbands and wives stating a proneness toward divorce.

In practical application, what does it mean when God is the center?

- Couples pray together.
- Couples read the Bible together.
- Couples attend church together.
- Both parties submit to God's leadership in their lives.

As time has passed in my own marriage, I've experienced God's strength in the center. When we argue, and yes we do argue, I tend to pray about it. So does Tim. As a result, I've been learning a kinder way to fight. God has been working on my heart and helping me to avoid being arrogant or obnoxious. These are two qualities I definitely possess.

I've also noticed that Tim apologizes or asks for forgiveness more readily. When we have calmed down, each of us often talk about how God helped us to seek a new way of solving our problems. It's nothing short of amazing.

If you are reading this choice, and you know your spouse doesn't share your faith in Christ, you can start by placing Him (Jesus) at the center of *your* life and *your* marital decision making.

Meanwhile, pray for your husband or wife.

From a strictly personal standpoint, making God the center has helped our marriage in ways I would have never imagined: anger issues, cleanliness, romance, communication style, parenting, and more.

Growth Questions:

- Do you know many people who have been divorced? What were their reasons for divorce?

- As you think about those reasons, with which topics could God grant a person wisdom and guidance?

- Have you committed to asking for God's guidance first in your life? Has your spouse? If you both trust Jesus completely, what's holding you back from asking Him to be the center of your marriage?

Bible verses on this topic:

"Glorify the Lord with me; let us exalt his name together." Psalm 34:3 (NIV)

"Seek first his kingdom and his righteousness and all these things will be added to you as well." Matthew 6:33 (NIV)

Similar choices:

#22 Sit on the Chair

#35 Devote Yourself to the Essentials

#16 Follow "The" Role Model

"Our greatest weakness lies in giving up.
The most certain way to succeed
is always to try just one more time."
~ Thomas A. Edison

REVERSE

If you missed something, or want to know these roads better, back up and try again. I don't know about you, but I often round the same corners everyday on my drives. Repetition builds skill.

[i] Stephen Pressfield. *The War of Art*. Black Irish Entertainment LLC. 2012

[ii] Parrot, Les and Leslie Parrot. "Bringing Laughter into Your Marriage," www.Focusonthefamily.com (from *The Love List*, Zondervan. 2002.)

[iii] Chapman, Gary. *The 5 Love Languages*. Northfield Publishing. New Edition 2009

[iv] Springer, Kate. "All You Need Is Love: Obama to Recognize Nation's Longest-Married Couple." Newsfeed.Time.com, February 1, 2012.

[v] Pearson, Jonathon."Fantasy World: Why are Boys Not Becoming Men?" JonathonPearson.com. May 31, 2012

[vi] Dr. Philipp G. Zimbardo and Nikita Duncan. "The Demise of Guys: How Video Games and Porn are Ruining a Generation." CNN Health, www.cnn.com. May 24, 2012.

[vii] Mary Kassian, "A Black and White Choice NOT to Read Fifty Shades of Grey," GirlsGoneWise.com, 2012.

[viii] Smith, Julien. *The Flinch*. The Domino Project. 2011.

[ix] Miller, Calvin. *The Empowered Communicator*. Broadman and Holman Pub. 1994.

[x] Maxwell, John. *Everyone Communicates, Few Connect*. Thomas Nelson. 2010.

[xi] Amato and Rogers (1997). Jeffrey P. Dew,"Financial issues as predictors of divorce." Paper presented at the annual conference of the National Council on Family Relations (November 2009). San Francisco, Ca.

[xii] The State of our Unions 2011. University of Virginia, National Marriage Project. 2011

Making Those Faithful Choices

This is me and my husband Tim. We've been married 16 years and want each of these faithful choices to fit our marriage, because we dream of sticking together for a lifetime.

Like you, we've got some corners we do well and others that require regular effort. I often need to turn around and try again. But, I believe our marriage is worth the effort.

We hope you join us as adventurers in marriage. Together, let's all spend our lives making faithful choices.

If you wish to read more choices connected to marriage, life, parenting or social media… stop by **www.FaithfulChoices.com** where we are helping couples find joy one faithful choice at a time.

Please share your review with others if you believe this book will help them too.

To invite Paula to come and speak to your church, school or organization on the topic of marriage email her Paula@FaithfulChoices.com.

Also available by Paula Whidden:
25 Days 'til Christ: An Advent Devotional for Families

"May you turn the roads of life together,
no matter what weather you face.
May each corner you reach provide a chance
to give each other grace.
If you pop a tire and pull to the side,
I pray you will see.
God will help you through this change,
just as He does for me."
~ Paula Whidden